W9-ABT-268

THE BENEDICTINE MEDAL

C.S.P.B.	Crux Sancti Patris Benedicti
	The Cross of our Holy Father Benedict
C.S.S.M.L.	Crux Sacra sit mihi lux
	May the Holy Cross be my light
N.D.S.M.D.	Ne Draco sit mihi dux
	Let not the devil be my guide

The outer letters stand for the words of an ancient verse:

V.R.S.	Vade retro Satana:
N.S.M.V.	numquam suade mihi vana.
S.M.Q.L.	Sunt mala quae libas;
I.V.B.	ipse venenum bibas.

Begone Satan
Never suggest vain things to me
what you offer is evil
drink your own poison.

SAINT BENEDICT'S PRAYER BOOK

Inspire among us, O Lord, that spirit to which
our Blessed Father Benedict was devoted. May
our community, filled with that same spirit, be
eager to love what he loved and in all our work
be faithful to his teaching.

*The quotations at the foot of each page are from
The Rule of Saint Benedict*

ACKNOWLEDGMENTS

Excerpts from the English translation of *The Roman Missal* © 1973, International Committee on English in the Liturgy, Inc. (ICEL); excerpts from the English translation of *Pastoral Care of the Sick: Rites of Anointing and Viaticum* © 1982, ICEL. All rights reserved.

Psalm texts, by permission of A.P. Watt Ltd on behalf of The Grail, England, from *The Psalms, A New Translation,* © 1963 The Grail, England, published by HarperCollins.

The passages from the *New Jerusalem Bible,* published and copyright 1985 Darton, Longman and Todd Ltd and Doubleday & Co Inc are used by permission of the publishers.

SAINT BENEDICT'S PRAYER BOOK FOR BEGINNERS

Ampleforth Abbey Press
(Distributed by Gracewing)

AMPLEFORTH ABBEY PRESS
AMPLEFORTH ABBEY
YORK

from

Gracewing
Fowler Wright Books
Southern Avenue, Leominster
Herefordshire HR6 0QF

Printed at The Cromwell Press

Typeset at Ampleforth College by Edward O'Malley

ISBN 0 85244 2580

First Reprint 1994
Second Reprint 1997

Imprimatur
DAVID C HOGAN
Middlesbrough
Chancellor

All rights reserved. No part of this publication may be reproduced, stored in a retrieval system, or transmitted in any form, or by any means, electronic, mechanical, photocopying, recording, or otherwise, without the written permission of the publisher.

© Ampleforth Abbey Trustees 1993

CONTENTS

CONTENTS

PROLOGUE

Some may think that the point of prayer is to get our own way with extra-terrestrial help, or to save us from facing the problems of life, or to provide an escape from 'reality', or to give an emotional uplift that makes you feel good. Some may think that prayer is a way of expanding our consciousness which is achieved by our own discipline and personal effort at self-improvement. These are caricatures of what Christian prayer really is. There may be a strand of truth in some of them, but they miss the real point of prayer.

To get to the true meaning of Christian prayer we have to go back to the beginning. We need first of all to face the truth, at once awesome and reassuring, that we are not alone in a time-bound universe; that another mode of being interpenetrates the life we live in sound and sight and sensation; that the very heart, in every sense of the word, of that other life is love. Thus St Paul (Gal:2) writes: "I am living here and now this mortal life, but my real life is the faith I have in the Son of God, who loved me and gave himself for me." That gives the clue to where Christian prayer begins. We are not crying out alone in uncomprehending darkness. We are called into communion with One who loves us. In responding through prayer we begin to find our way to a love beyond imagining. That is what prayer is about.

The next point is that the further we are from seeing things as St Paul saw them, the greater is our need of prayer. We need the gift-love of God because without it we sink into spiritual death; and prayer is the only way to open our hearts to that love. It is the response God asks of us and for which he waits with infinite patience. We never can appreciate love by neglecting it, by turning away from it. And it rests with us to open the door to that love, admitting it with its gifts and demands into our lives. It is through prayer that every day we may open the door a little wider and come a little nearer to understanding who we are and what our lives are really for.

This prayer book is to help anyone who comes across it in that daily pilgrimage. The prayers and texts in it rely on the special means that have been given us in the great Catholic tradition; they rely on the word of God in scripture, on the sacraments, on traditional devotions of the Church, on the prayers of saints. These are the prayer-centred gifts by which we are helped to open the door to God's love in our lives. We should think carefully, then, on how best to use them. Remember that the words are nothing in themselves. Words can be recited with our minds far away. It is the meaning that matters and calls for our attention. Yet even the meaning is not enough for the fullness of prayer. It is possible to take the meaning of a prayer or text of scripture and think about it, analyse it, criticise it without ever letting it penetrate our heart and spiritual consciousness. But that penetration is what we need; it is the true purpose of prayer.

To bring prayers to life, then we must give time for the meaning to sink in. It is good to pause between prayers and readings and above all to listen carefully in our heart for what the words say to us at this moment at which we pray. For those who listen prayer is never a one-way traffic, especially in the reading of the word of God in scripture. If we listen "with the ears of the heart," as St Benedict put it, the word of God comes to us here and now to teach and guide and His love touches our individual lives. It makes all the difference, if we are attentive and spiritually on the alert in prayer.

To illustrate such an approach let us take, as a random example, Morning Prayer for Wednesday of Week One. It begins with a short prayer to offer the day to God Our Father. We offer to Him ourselves and the day to come, but the point of the prayer is in our personal surrender to God's love as this day begins; the words of this prayer will help and guide, but the true act is within; the more genuine, the more loving, the more personal it is, the more fruitful is the prayer in our hearts. The prayer is realistic; it mentions sufferings, disappointments, joys; whichever predominates will colour the prayer and bring it to life. We have started with our real self in a real offering in a particular situation on a particular day.

After that comes the great psalm 138 about God's providence. We are lifted by it into a world in which we share with all God's children a perception (given us through His word in scripture) of His guiding hand. Using words that saints have used through the ages, words that Christ himself used on earth, words that bring to our individual lives a timeless cutting edge, we recognise our utter dependence on God in life and death. After that comes a reading from Hebrews which takes up the theme of our nakedness before God, but it does not leave us there. It turns to focus on the ground of our hope and confidence, that is to our faith in Christ and the forgiveness and salvation he brings: "Let us, then, have no fear in approaching the throne of grace." Thus we are led in our prayer by the word of God. Everyone who listens "with the ears of the heart" will find his or her own special inspiration for the day in some word or phrase from the psalm or reading. That is how the word of God sustains and guides us in our prayer.

We are ready now for the first of all prayers. It was given us by Christ in the gospel - the Our Father. It expresses all our deepest needs. It ends with the most urgent of all in the plea that we should be delivered from the evil which threatens us daily. Words, that are not ours but are given to us, say for us what we most need to say - ask for us what we most need to ask. With that, we turn to ask Our Lady in the Hail Mary for the care of a mother in whatever we face today.

PROLOGUE

Our morning prayer is nearly complete and we move to the final prayer. That passage from Hebrews has reminded us how Christ identifies with us in our greatest need. It gives us courage to end with a prayer that God will see Christ in us and lead us to share his life.

Such a morning prayer is not a bad way to begin any day. It leads us through the word of God to discover his love and make it real in our lives. That is what prayer should be - a dialogue of love. As we try to make it our own there will be many obstacles: distractions, laziness, ambition, the dullness of life or the excitement of life, the pleasure, the happiness, the hardship that we meet with, the suffering, the pain, the disappointment. We should never let them discourage us or turn us away from prayer. They are part of our lives and so they are part also of our offering, of our repentance, of our thanksgiving; as such they are all an essential part of our prayer to God our Father so that he may heal us, confirm us in good, draw us closer to him, and give us the intimate guidance we need in life. What are called distractions in prayer can thus be turned into part of our self-offering. The gentle discipline of this beginner's book will help us on the way. It is for everyone of every age, because we are all beginners in prayer. This must be true since the end of prayer is here and beyond, now and always; its perspective begins in time and is lost to our comprehending in God and eternity.

ALWAYS
WE
BEGIN
AGAIN

SUNDAY

Morning Offering

Grant, O Lord,
that none may love you less this day because of me;
that never word or act of mine
may turn one soul from thee;
and, ever daring, yet one more grace would I implore,
that many souls this day,
because of me, may love thee more. Amen.

Psalm 150

Praise God in his holy place,
praise him in his mighty heavens.
Praise him for his powerful deeds,
praise his surpassing greatness.

O praise him with sound of trumpet,
praise him with lute and harp.
Praise him with timbrel and dance,
praise him with strings and pipes.

O praise him with resounding cymbals,
praise him with clashing of cymbals.
Let everything that lives and that breathes
give praise to the Lord.
Alleluia!

---

*Listen carefully, my son, to the master's instructions, and
attend to them with the ear of your heart.*

Reading   *1 Cor 15: 51-55*

Now I am going to tell you a mystery:
  we are not all going to fall asleep,
  but we are all going to be changed, instantly,
  in the twinkling of an eye
  when the last trumpet sounds.
The trumpet is going to sound,
  and then the dead will be raised, imperishable,
  and we shall be changed.
Because this perishable nature of ours
  must put on imperishability
  this mortal nature must put on immortality.
  And after this perishable nature
  has put on imperishability,
  and this mortal nature has put on immortality,
  then will the words of scripture come true:
  Death is swallowed up in victory.
Death where is your victory?
  Death where is your sting?

Our Father... Hail Mary...

The labour of obedience will bring you back to him from
whom you had drifted through the sloth of disobedience.

Concluding Prayer

Father, in the rising of your Son
death gives birth to new life.
The sufferings he endured
restored hope to a fallen world.
Let sin never ensnare us
with empty promises of passing joy.
Make us one with you always,
so that our joy may be holy,
and our love may give life.
Through Christ our Lord. Amen.

Every time you begin a good work, you must pray to him
most earnestly to bring it to perfection.

MONDAY

Morning Offering

Father, we offer to you this day
all our thoughts, words and actions,
all our sufferings and disappointments,
and all our joys.
And we unite our lives
with that of your beloved Son, Jesus Christ. Amen.

Psalm 83

How lovely is your dwelling place,
Lord, God of hosts.

My soul is longing and yearning,
is yearning for the courts of the Lord.
My heart and my soul ring out their joy
to God, the living God.

The sparrow herself finds a home
and the swallow a nest for her brood;
she lays her young by your altars,
Lord of hosts, my king and my God.

---

*In his goodness he has already counted us as his sons, and
therefore we should never grieve him by our evil actions.*

Reading   *Col 3: 1-4,12-14*

Since you have been raised up to be with Christ,
 you must look for the things that are above,
 where Christ is, sitting at God's right hand.
Let your thought be on things above,
 not on the things that are on the earth,
because you have died,
 and now the life you have
 is hidden with Christ in God.
But when Christ is revealed -
 and he is your life -
 you, too, will be revealed with him in glory.
As the chosen of God, then,
 the holy people whom he loves,
 you are to be clothed in heartfelt compassion,
 in generosity and humility,
 gentleness and patience.
Bear with one another;
 forgive each other
 if one of you has a complaint against another.
The Lord has forgiven you;
 now you must do the same.
Over all these clothes, put on love,
 the perfect bond.

Our Father... Hail Mary...

Let us open our eyes to the light that comes from God.

Concluding Prayer

Father in heaven,
the hand of your loving kindness
powerfully yet gently guides
all the moments of our day.
Go before us in our pilgrimage of life,
anticipate our needs and prevent our failing.
Send your Spirit to unite us in faith,
that sharing in your service
we may rejoice in your presence.
Through Christ our Lord. Amen.

See how the Lord in his love shows us the way of life.

TUESDAY

Morning Offering

Father,
you have brought us to the beginning of a new day.
Your hand is upon us to care for and protect us.
We offer you our lives and hearts.
May we always do your will
and love our neighbour as ourselves. Amen.

Psalm 42

Defend me, O God, and plead my cause
against a godless nation.
From deceitful and cunning men
rescue me, O God.

O send forth your light and your truth;
let these be my guide.
Let them bring me to your holy mountain
to the place where you dwell.

And I will come to the altar of God,
the God of my joy.
My redeemer, I will thank you on the harp,
O God, my God.

---

*If we wish to dwell in the tent of this kingdom, we will
never arrive unless we run there by doing good deeds.*

Why are you cast down, my soul,
why groan within me?
Hope in God; I will praise him still,
my saviour and my God.

Reading   *1 Cor 12: 4-6,12-13,27*

There are many different gifts,
    but it is always the same Spirit;
    there are many different ways of serving,
    but it is always the same Lord.
There are many different forms of activity,
    but in everybody it is the same God
    who is at work in them all.
The particular manifestation of the Spirit
    granted to each one
    is to be used for the general good.
For as with the human body
    which is a unity although it has many parts -
    all the parts of the body, though many,
    still making up one body -
    so it is with Christ.
We were baptised into one body in a single Spirit,
    and we were all given the same Spirit to drink.
Now Christ's body is yourselves,
    each of you with a part to play in the whole.

Our Father... Hail Mary...

---

*They do not become elated over their good deeds; they judge it is the
Lord's power, not their own, that brings about the good in them.*

Concluding Prayer

Lord God of power and might,
nothing is good which is against your will,
and all is of value which comes from your hand.
Place in our hearts a desire to please you
and fill our minds with insight into love,
so that every thought may grow in wisdom
and all our efforts may be filled with your peace.
Through Christ our Lord. Amen.

The Lord waits for us daily to translate into action, as we should, his holy teachings.

WEDNESDAY

Morning Offering

Father, we offer to you this day
all our thoughts, words and actions,
all our sufferings and disappointments,
and all our joys.
And we unite our lives
with that of your beloved Son, Jesus Christ. Amen.

Psalm 138 (Part 1)

O Lord, you search me and you know me,
you know my resting and my rising,
you discern my purpose from afar.
You mark when I walk or lie down,
all my ways lie open to you.

Before ever a word is on my tongue
you know it, O Lord, through and through.
Behind and before you besiege me,
your hand ever laid upon me.
Too wonderful for me, this knowledge,
too high, beyond my reach.

O where can I go from your spirit,
or where can I flee from your face?
If I climb the heavens, you are there.
If I lie in the grave, you are there.

---

*We must prepare our hearts and bodies for the battle of
holy obedience.*

If I take the wings of the dawn
and dwell at the sea's furthest end,
even there your hand would lead me,
your right hand would hold me fast.

Reading   *Heb 4: 12-16*

The word of God is something alive and active:
  it cuts more incisively than any two-edged sword:
  it can seek out the place
  where soul is divided from spirit,
  or joints from marrow;
  it can pass judgement
  on secret emotions and thoughts.
No created thing is hidden from him;
  everything is uncovered and stretched fully open
  to the eyes of the one to whom we must give
  account of ourselves.
Since in Jesus, the Son of God,
  we have the supreme high priest
  who has gone through to the highest heaven,
  we must hold firm to our profession of faith.
For the high priest we have
  is not incapable of feeling our weaknesses with us,
  but has been put to the test
  in exactly the same way as ourselves,
  apart from sin.
Let us, then, have no fear
  in approaching the throne of grace.

*What is not possible to us by nature, let us ask the Lord to
supply by the help of his grace.*

Our Father... Hail Mary...

Concluding Prayer

Almighty God, accept our adoration and our praise.
See and love in us what you see and love in your Son,
who is true man and true God.
By your goodness, lead us to a share in his divinity,
who humbled himself to share in our humanity.
We ask this through Christ our Lord. Amen.

We must do now what will profit us forever.

THURSDAY

Morning Offering

Father,
you have brought us to the beginning of a new day.
Your hand is upon us to care for and protect us.
We offer you our lives and hearts.
May we always do your will
and love our neighbour as ourselves. Amen.

Psalm 137

I thank you, Lord, with all my heart,
you have heard the words of my mouth.
In the presence of the angels I will bless you.
I will adore before your holy temple.

I thank you for your faithfulness and love
which excel all we ever knew of you.
On the day I called, you answered;
you increased the strength of my soul.

The Lord is high yet he looks on the lowly
and the haughty he knows from afar.
Though I walk in the midst of affliction
you give me life and frustrate my foes.

---

*The good of all concerned may prompt us to a little
strictness in order to amend faults and to safeguard love.*

You stretch out your hand and save me,
your hand will do all things for me.
Your love, O Lord, is eternal;
discard not the works of your hands.

Reading   *1 Cor 11: 23-29*

The tradition I received from the Lord
    and also handed on to you
    is that on the night he was betrayed,
    the Lord Jesus took some bread,
    and after he had given thanks, he broke it,
    and he said,
'This is my body, which is for you;
    do this in remembrance of me.'
And in the same way,
    with the cup after supper, saying,
    'This cup is the new covenant in my blood.
    Whenever you drink it,
    do this as a memorial of me.'
Whenever you eat this bread, then, and drink this cup,
    you are proclaiming the Lord's death
    until he comes.
Therefore anyone who eats the bread
    or drinks the cup of the Lord unworthily
    is answerable for the body and blood of the Lord.

Our Father... Hail Mary...

---

*We shall run on the path of God's commandments, our
hearts overflowing with the inexpressible delight of love.*

Concluding Prayer

God our Father,
open our eyes to see your hand at work
in the splendour of creation,
in the beauty of human life.
Touched by your hand our world is holy.
Help us to cherish the gifts that surround us,
to share your blessings with our brothers and sisters,
and to experience the joy of life in your presence.
Through Christ our Lord. Amen.

*We shall through patience share in the sufferings of Christ,
that we may deserve also to share in his kingdom.*

FRIDAY

Morning Offering

O my God, I offer you
all my thoughts, words, actions,
and sufferings;
and I beseech you to give me your grace
that I may not offend you this day,
but may faithfully serve you
and do your holy will in all things. Amen.

Psalm 50

Have mercy on me, God, in your kindness.
In your compassion blot out my offence.
O wash me more and more from my guilt
and cleanse me from my sin.

My offences truly I know them;
my sin is always before me.
Against you, you alone, have I sinned;
what is evil in your sight I have done.

Indeed you love truth in the heart;
then in the secret of my heart teach me wisdom.
O purify me, then I shall be clean;
O wash me, I shall be whiter than snow.

---

*He must point out all that is good and holy more by
example than by words.*

Make me hear rejoicing and gladness,
that the bones you have crushed you may thrill.

O rescue me, God my helper,
and my tongue shall ring out your goodness.
O Lord, open my lips
and my mouth shall declare your praise.

Reading   *James 2: 14-20, 24, 26*

How does it help, my brothers, when someone
    who has never done a single good act
    claims to have faith?
Will that faith bring salvation?
If one of the brothers or one of the sisters
    is in need of clothes
    and has not enough food to live on,
    and one of you says to him,
    'I wish you well;
    keep yourself warm and eat plenty,'
    without giving him these bare necessities of life,
    then what good is that?
In the same way faith:
    if good deeds do not go with it, it is quite dead.
You believe in the one God - that is creditable enough,
    but even the demons have the same belief,
    and they tremble with fear.

---

*Only in this are we distinguished in his sight: if we are
found better than others in good works and in humility.*

31

It is by deeds, and not only by believing,
    that someone is justified.
As a body without a spirit is dead,
    so is faith without deeds.

Our Father... Hail Mary...

Concluding Prayer

Almighty Father, remember the love you have for us.
May the suffering and death of your Son
remind us of the greatness of your wisdom,
prompt us to repay your love with obedience,
and teach us how to love one another as he loved us.
Through Christ our Lord. Amen.

More will be expected of a man to whom more has been entrusted.

SATURDAY

Morning Offering

O Jesus, through the most pure heart of Mary,
I offer you all the prayers, works,
sufferings and joys of this day,
for the intentions of your Divine Heart. Amen.

Psalm 8

How great is your name, O Lord our God,
through all the earth!

Your majesty is praised above the heavens;
on the lips of children and of babes
you have found praise to foil your enemy,
to silence the foe and the rebel.

When I see the heavens, the work of your hands,
the moon and the stars which you arranged,
what is man that you should keep him in mind,
mortal man that you care for him?

Yet you have made him little less than a God;
with glory and honour you crowned him,
gave him power over the works of your hand,
put all things under his feet.

Above all, he must not show too great concern for the
fleeting and temporal things of this world.

All of them, sheep and cattle,
yes, even the savage beasts,
birds of the air, and fish
that make their way through the waters.
How great is your name, O Lord our God,
through all the earth!

Reading   *Gal 5: 17-23,25*

The desires of self-indulgence
    are always in opposition to the Spirit,
    and the desires of the Spirit
    are in opposition to self-indulgence;
    they are opposites, one against the other.
When self-indulgence is at work
    the results are obvious;
    sexual vice, impurity and sensuality,
    the worship of false gods and sorcery,
    antagonisms and rivalry,
    jealousy, bad temper and quarrels,
    disagreements, factions and malice,
    drunkenness, orgies and all such things.
And about these, I tell you now
    as I have told you in the past,
    that people who behave in these ways
    will not inherit the Kingdom of God.

The Lord often reveals what is better to the younger.

On the other hand, the fruit of the Spirit
    is love, joy, peace,
    patience, kindness, goodness,
    trustfulness, gentleness and self-control;
    no law can touch such things as these.
Since we are living by the Spirit,
    let our behaviour be guided by the Spirit.

Our Father... Hail Mary...

Concluding Prayer

Almighty Father, the love you offer
is always greater than anything we could hope for,
because you are greater than the human heart.
Direct each thought, each effort today,
so that the limits of our faults and weaknesses
may not obscure the vision of your glory,
nor keep us from the peace you have promised.
Through Christ our Lord. Amen.

Do not pamper yourself.

SUNDAY

Morning Offering

Grant, O Lord,
that none may love you less this day because of me;
that never word or act of mine
may turn one soul from thee;
and, ever daring, yet one more grace would I implore,
that many souls this day,
because of me, may love thee more. Amen.

Psalm 148

Praise the Lord from the heavens,
praise him in the heights.
Praise him, all his angels,
praise him, all his host.

Praise him, sun and moon,
praise him, shining stars.
Praise him, highest heavens
and the waters above the heavens.

Praise the Lord from the earth,
sea creatures and all oceans,
fire and hail, snow and mist,
stormy winds that obey his word;

Go to help the troubled and console the sorrowing.

all mountains and hills,
all fruit trees and cedars,
beasts, wild and tame,
reptiles and birds on the wing;
all earth's kings and peoples,
earth's princes and rulers;
young men and maidens,
old men together with children.

Reading   *1 Cor 15: 20-26*

Christ has been raised from the dead,
    as the first-fruits of all who have fallen asleep.
As it was by one man that death came,
    so through one man
    has come the resurrection of the dead.
Just as all die in Adam,
    so in Christ all will be brought to life;
    but all of them in their proper order:
    Christ the first-fruits,
    and next, at his coming, those who belong to him.
After that will come the end,
    when he will hand over the kingdom
    to God the Father,
    having abolished every principality,
    every ruling force and power.

Your way of acting should be different from the world's way.

For he is to be king
    until he has made his enemies his footstool,
    and the last of the enemies
    to be done away with is death,
    for he has put all things under his feet.

Our Father... Hail Mary...

Concluding Prayer

Heavenly Father,
we rejoice today in the resurrection of your Son.
Through his obedience,
your love re-opened the gates of heaven for us,
and gained for us a reward for faith so wonderful
that no human eye has seen, no human ear has heard,
no human spirit ever guessed at how wonderful it is.
Keep us faithful to you,
and make us worthy of the promises of Christ,
through whom we make this prayer. Amen.

The love of Christ must come before all else.

MONDAY

Morning Offering

Father, we offer to you this day
all our thoughts, words and actions,
all our sufferings and disappointments, and all our joys.
And we unite our lives
with that of your beloved Son, Jesus Christ. Amen.

Psalm 97

Sing a new song to the Lord
for he has worked wonders.
His right hand and his holy arm
have brought salvation.

The Lord has made known his salvation;
has shown his justice to the nations.
He has remembered his truth and his love
for the house of Israel.

All the ends of the world have seen
the salvation of our God.
Shout to the Lord all the earth,
ring out your joy.

Rejoice at the presence of the Lord:
for he comes to rule the earth.
He will rule the world with justice
and the peoples with fairness.

You are not to act in anger or nurse a grudge.

Reading   *2 Peter 1:3-8,11*

By his divine power,
 he has lavished on us all the things we need
 for life and for true devotion,
 through the knowledge of him who has called us
 by his own glory and goodness.
Through these, the greatest and priceless promises
 have been lavished on us,
 that through them
 you should share the divine nature
 and escape the corruption rife in the world
 through disordered passion.
With this in view, do your utmost
 to support your faith with goodness,
 goodness with understanding,
 understanding with self-control,
 self-control with perseverance,
 perseverance with devotion,
 devotion with kindness to the brothers,
 and kindness to the brothers with love.
The possession and growth of these qualities
 will prevent your knowledge
 of our Lord Jesus Christ
 from being ineffectual or unproductive.

Rid your heart of all deceit.

In this way you will be given the generous gift
    of entry to the eternal kingdom
    of our Lord and Saviour Jesus Christ.

Our Father... Hail Mary...

Concluding Prayer

Lord our God, Father of all,
you guard us under the shadow of your wings
and search into the depths of our hearts.
Remove the blindness that cannot know you
and relieve the fear
that would hide us from your sight.
Through Christ our Lord. Amen.

---

*Never give a hollow greeting of peace or turn away when
someone needs your love.*

TUESDAY

Morning Offering

Father,
you have brought us to the beginning of a new day.
Your hand is upon us to care for and protect us.
We offer you our lives and hearts.
May we always do your will
and love our neighbour as ourselves. Amen.

Psalm 120

I lift up my eyes to the mountains:
from where shall come my help?
My help shall come from the Lord
who made heaven and earth.

May he never allow you to stumble!
Let him sleep not, your guard.
No, he sleeps not nor slumbers,
Israel's guard.

The Lord is your guard and your shade;
at your right side he stands.
By day the sun shall not smite you
nor the moon in the night.

Speak the truth with heart and tongue.

The Lord will guard you from evil,
he will guard your soul.
The Lord will guard your going and coming
both now and for ever.

Reading   *Romans 8: 26-30*

The Spirit comes to help us in our weakness,
    for, when we do not know how to pray properly,
    then the Spirit personally
    makes our petitions for us
    in groans that cannot be put into words;
and he who can see into all hearts
    knows what the Spirit means
    because the prayers that the Spirit makes
    for God's holy people
    are always in accordance with the mind of God.
We are well aware that God works
    with those who love him,
    those who have been called
    in accordance with his purpose,
    and turns everything to their good.
He decided beforehand, who were the ones
    destined to be moulded to the pattern of his Son,
    so that he should be the eldest of many brothers;

Do not injure anyone, but bear injuries patiently.

it was those so destined that he called;
    those that he called, he justified,
    and those that he has justified
    he has brought into glory.

Our Father... Hail Mary...

Concluding Prayer

Lord our God, all truth is from you,
and you alone bring oneness of heart.
Give your people the joy of hearing your word
and of longing for your presence
more than for life itself.
May all the attractions of a changing world
serve only to make us value more
the peace of your kingdom
which this world does not give.
Through Christ our Lord. Amen.

If people curse you, do not curse them back but bless them instead.

WEDNESDAY

Morning Offering

Father, we offer to you this day
all our thoughts, words and actions,
all our sufferings and disappointments,
and all our joys.
And we unite our lives
with that of your beloved Son, Jesus Christ. Amen.

Psalm 26

The Lord is my light and my help;
whom shall I fear?
The Lord is the stronghold of my life;
before whom shall I shrink?

Though an army encamp against me
my heart would not fear.
Though war break out against me
even then would I trust.

There is one thing I ask of the Lord,
for this I long, to live in the house of the Lord,
all the days of my life,
to savour the sweetness of the Lord,
to behold his temple.

Refrain from too much eating or sleeping.

I am sure I shall see the Lord's goodness
in the land of the living.
Hope in him, hold firm and take heart.
Hope in the Lord!

Reading   *Romans 12: 2-6*

Do not model yourself
    on the behaviour of the world around you,
    but let your behaviour change,
    modelled by your new mind.
This is the only way to discover the will of God
    and know what is good,
    what it is that God wants,
    what is the perfect thing to do.
In the light of the grace I have received
    I want to urge each one among you
    not to exaggerate his real importance.
Each of you must judge himself soberly
    by the standard of the faith God has given him.
Just as each of our bodies has several parts
    and each part has a separate function,
    so all of us, in union with Christ, form one body,
    and as parts of it we all belong to each other.
Our gifts differ according to the grace given us.

Our Father... Hail Mary...

Do not grumble or speak ill of others.

Concluding Prayer

Father in heaven, open our hearts to your wisdom.
Teach us how to look for dignity in humility,
how to find opportunities for love in service,
so that we may share in the peace of Christ
who offered his life in the service of all.
Through Christ our Lord. Amen.

Place your hope in God alone.

THURSDAY

Morning Offering

Father,
you have brought us to the beginning of a new day.
Your hand is upon us to care for and protect us.
We offer you our lives and hearts.
May we always do your will
and love our neighbour as ourselves. Amen.

Psalm 126

If the Lord does not build the house,
in vain do its builders labour;
if the Lord does not watch over the city,
in vain does the watchman keep vigil.

In vain is your earlier rising,
your going later to rest,
you who toil for the bread you eat:
when he pours gifts on his beloved
while they slumber.

Truly sons are a gift from the Lord,
a blessing, the fruit of the womb.
Indeed the sons of youth
are like arrows in the hand of a warrior.

---

*If you notice something good in yourself, give credit to God,
not to yourself.*

O the happiness of the man
who has filled his quiver with these arrows!
He will have no cause for shame
when he disputes with his foes in the gateways.

Reading   *Romans 5: 1–2, 6, 8, 10–11*

Now that we have been justified by faith,
    we are at peace with God
      through our Lord Jesus Christ;
      it is through him, by faith,
      that we have been admitted into God's favour
    in which we are living.
    and look forward exultantly to God's glory.
For when we were still helpless,
    at the appointed time, Christ died for the godless.
So it is proof of God's own love for us
    that Christ died for us while we were still sinners.
If, while we were enemies,
    we were reconciled to God
      through the death of his Son,
    how much more can we be sure
    that, being now reconciled,
    we shall be saved by his life.

Be certain that the evil you commit is always your own and
yours to acknowledge.

What is more, we are filled with exultant trust in God,
    through our Lord Jesus Christ,
    through whom we have already gained
    our reconciliation.

Our Father... Hail Mary...

Concluding Prayer

Father, let the gift of your life
continue to grow in us,
drawing us from death to faith, hope and love.
Keep us alive in Christ Jesus.
Keep us watchful in prayer and true to his teaching
till your glory is revealed in us.
Through Christ our Lord. Amen.

Live in fear of judgment day.

FRIDAY

Morning Offering

O my God, I offer you
all my thoughts, words, actions, and sufferings;
and I beseech you to give me your grace
that I may not offend you this day,
but may faithfully serve you
and do your holy will in all things. Amen.

Psalm 118: 105-112

I call with all my heart; Lord, hear me,
I will keep your commands.
I call upon you, save me
and I will do your will.

I rise before dawn and cry for help,
I hope in your word.
My eyes watch through the night
to ponder your promise.

In your love hear my voice, O Lord;
give me life by your decrees.
Those who harm me unjustly draw near:
they are far from your law.

Have a great horror of hell.

But you, O Lord, are close:
your commands are truth.
Long have I known that your will
is established for ever.

Reading   *Romans 6: 3-4,8-11*

You cannot have forgotten that all of us,
    when we were baptised into Christ Jesus,
    were baptised into his death.
So by our baptism into his death
    we were buried with him,
    so that as Christ was raised from the dead
    by the Father's glorious power,
    we too should begin living a new life.
We believe that, if we died with Christ,
    then we shall live with him too.
We know that Christ has been raised from the dead,
    and will never die again.
Death has no power over him any more.
For by dying, he is dead to sin once and for all,
    and now the life that he lives is life with God.
In the same way,
    you must see yourselves as being dead to sin
    but alive for God in Christ Jesus.

Our Father... Hail Mary...

Yearn for everlasting life with holy desire.

Concluding Prayer

God our Father,
you are slow to anger and rich in mercy.
By the power of your Son's blood,
you take away our sins,
and redeem us from death.
Fill us with gratitude for his sacrifice,
renew our faith, and soften our hearts
so that we may learn to love you with all our strength
and all our heart and all our soul,
and our neighbour as ourselves.
We ask this through Christ our Lord. Amen.

Day by day remind yourself that you are going to die.

SATURDAY

Morning Offering

O Jesus, through the most pure heart of Mary,
I offer you all the prayers, works,
sufferings and joys of this day,
for the intentions of your Divine Heart. Amen.

Psalm 115

I trusted even when I said:
"I am sorely afflicted,"
and when I said in my alarm:
"No man can be trusted."

How can I repay the Lord
for his goodness to me?
The cup of salvation I will raise;
I will call on the Lord's name.

My vows to the Lord I will fulfil
before all his people.
O precious in the eyes of the Lord
is the death of his faithful.

Your servant, Lord, your servant am I;
you have loosened my bonds.
A thanksgiving sacrifice I make:
I will call on the Lord's name.

---

*Hour by hour keep careful watch over all you do, aware that
God's gaze is upon you, wherever you may be.*

My vows to the Lord I will fulfil
before all his people,
in the courts of the house of the Lord,
in your midst, O Jerusalem.

Reading   *Eph 3: 14–21*

This, then, is what I pray,
    kneeling before the Father,
    from whom every fatherhood,
    in heaven or on earth, takes its name.
In the abundance of his glory may he,
    through his Spirit,
    enable you to grow firm in power
    with regard to your inner self,
    so that Christ may live in your hearts
    through faith,
and then, planted in love and built on love,
    with all God's holy people
    you will have the strength to grasp
    the breadth and the length,
    the height and the depth;
so that, knowing the love of Christ
    which is beyond knowledge,
    you may be filled with the utter fullness of God.

---

*As soon as wrongful thoughts come into your heart, dash them
against Christ.*

Glory to him whose power, working in us,
    can do infinitely more
    than we can ask or imagine;
glory be to him from generation to generation,
    in the Church and in Christ Jesus
    for ever and ever. Amen.

Our Father... Hail Mary...

Concluding Prayer

Father in heaven,
form in us the likeness of your Son
and deepen his life within us.
Send us as witnesses of gospel joy
into a world of fragile peace and broken promises.
Touch all hearts with your love
so we may, in turn, love each other.
Through Christ our Lord. Amen.

Guard your lips from harmful or deceptive speech.

SUNDAY

Prayer of Thanksgiving

We give you thanks and praise, Almighty Father,
for having called us today to celebrate
the eternal covenant of our redemption.
Make this evening holy,
and never withdraw your love from us.
Through Christ our Lord.

Psalm 114

I love the Lord for he has heard
the cry of my appeal;
for he turned his ear to me
in the day when I called him.

They surrounded me, the snares of death,
with the anguish of the tomb;
they caught me, sorrow and distress.
I called on the Lord's name.
O Lord my God, deliver me!

How gracious is the Lord, and just;
our God has compassion.
The Lord protects the simple hearts;
I was helpless so he saved me.

Prefer moderation in speech and speak no foolish chatter.

Turn back, my soul, to your rest
for the Lord has been good;
he has kept my soul from death,
my eyes from tears
and my feet from stumbling.

I will walk in the presence of the Lord
in the land of the living.

Reading
Heb 12: 18-19,22-24,28

What you have come to
　　is nothing known to the senses;
　　not a blazing fire, or gloom, or total darkness,
　　or a storm, or trumpet blast,
　　or the sound of a voice speaking
　　which made everyone that heard it
　　beg that no more should be said to them.
But what you have come to is Mount Zion
　　and the city of the living God,
　　the heavenly Jerusalem
　　where the millions of angels
　　have gathered for the festival,
　　with the whole Church of first-born sons,
　　enrolled as citizens of heaven.

Listen readily to holy reading.

You have come to God himself, the supreme Judge,
    and to the spirits of the upright
    who have been made perfect;
    and to Jesus, the mediator of a new covenant,
    and to purifying blood
    which pleads more insistently than Abel's.
We have been given possession
    of an unshakeable kingdom.

Our Father... Hail Mary...

Concluding Prayer

O Lord, support us all the day long
until the shades lengthen and the evening comes,
and the busy world is hushed,
and the fever of life is over,
and our work is done.
Then, Lord, in your mercy,
grant us a safe lodging, and peace at the last. Amen.

Devote yourself often to prayer.

MONDAY

Prayer of Thanksgiving

Thank you Lord
for the love and protection
you have shown us throughout this day.
Stretch your hand of blessing over us this evening
that we may end the day as we began it,
by praising your holy name.
Through Christ our Lord. Amen.

Psalm 41

Like the deer that yearns
for running streams,
so my soul is yearning
for you, my God.

My soul is thirsting for God,
the God of my life;
when can I enter and see
the face of God?

Why are you cast down, my soul,
why groan within me?
Hope in God, I will praise him still,
my saviour and my God.

---

*Every day with tears and sighs confess your past sins to God
in prayer.*

By day the Lord will send
his loving kindness;
by night I will sing to him,
praise the God of my life.

Reading   *Eph 1: 3-10*

Blessed be God the Father of our Lord Jesus Christ
    who has blessed us
      with all the spiritual blessings of heaven in Christ.
Thus he chose us in Christ before the world was made
    to be holy and faultless before him in love,
    marking us out for himself beforehand,
    to be adopted sons, through Jesus Christ.
Such was his purpose and good pleasure,
    to the praise of the glory of his grace,
    his free gift to us in the Beloved,
    in whom, through his blood,
    we gain our freedom,
    the forgiveness of our sins.
Such is the richness of his grace
    which he has showered on us,
    in all wisdom and insight.

Hate the urgings of self-will.

He has let us know the mystery of his purpose,
    according to his good pleasure
    which he determined beforehand in Christ,
    for him to act upon
    when the times had run their course:
    that he would bring everything together
    under Christ as head,
    everything in the heaven and everything on earth.

Our Father... Hail Mary...

Concluding Prayer

Take Lord, all my liberty.
Receive my memory, my understanding,
and my whole will.
Whatever I have and possess, you have given me;
to you I restore it wholly and to your will
I utterly surrender it for my direction.
Give me the love of you only,
with your grace, and I am rich enough,
nor do I ask anything beside. Amen.

Do not aspire to be called holy before you really are.

TUESDAY

Prayer of Thanksgiving

Almighty Father, in your loving providence
every hair of our head is counted,
every tear is noted, and every prayer heard.
We thank you for your faithful goodness to us,
and ask for a peaceful evening, and blessed rest.
Through Christ our Lord. Amen.

Psalm 62

O God, you are my God, for you I long;
for you my soul is thirsting.
My body pines for you
like a dry, weary land without water.
So I gaze on you in the sanctuary
to see your strength and your glory.

For your love is better than life,
my lips will speak your praise.
So I will bless you all my life,
in your name I will lift up my hands.
My soul shall be filled as with a banquet,
my mouth shall praise you with joy.

Live by God's commandments every day.

On my bed I remember you.
On you I muse through the night
for you have been my help;
in the shadow of your wings I rejoice.
My soul clings to you;
your right hand holds me fast.

Reading   Col 1: 15-20

He is the image of the unseen God,
    the first-born of all creation,
for in him were created all things
    in heaven and on earth:
    everything visible and everything invisible,
    thrones, ruling forces, sovereignties, powers -
    all things were created through him and for him.
He exists before all things
    and in him all things hold together,
and he is the Head of the Body,
    that is, the Church.
He is the Beginning,
    the first-born from the dead,
    so that he should be supreme in every way;
because God wanted all fullness to be found in him
    and through him to reconcile all things to him,
    everything in heaven and everything on earth,
    by making peace through his death on the cross.

Our Father... Hail Mary...

---

*Harbour neither hatred nor jealousy of anyone, and do
nothing out of envy.*

Concluding Prayer

May the Lord bless us and keep us.
May the Lord let his face shine on us
and be gracious to us.
May the Lord show us his face
and bring us peace. Amen.

Do not love quarrelling.

WEDNESDAY

Prayer of Thanksgiving

We give you thanks, almighty God,
for all the gifts you have given us during this day.
Keep our hearts open to your love and grace this
evening, that we may always deserve to be called your
children. Through Christ our Lord. Amen.

Psalm 138 (Part 2)

It was you who created my being,
knit me together in my mother's womb.
I thank you for the wonder of my being,
for the wonders of all your creation.

Already you knew my soul,
my body held no secret from you
when I was being fashioned in secret
and moulded in the depths of the earth.

Your eyes saw all my actions,
they were all of them written in your book;
every one of my days was decreed
before one of them came into being.

To me, how mysterious your thoughts,
the sum of them not to be numbered!
If I count them, they are more than the sand;
to finish, I must be eternal, like you.

Shun arrogance.

O search me, God, and know my heart.
O test me and know my thoughts.
See that I follow not the wrong path
and lead me in the path of life eternal.

Reading   *1 John 4: 7-12*

My dear friends,
    let us love each other,
    since love is from God
    and everyone who loves is a child of God
    and knows God.
Whoever fails to love
    does not know God,
    because God is love.
This is the revelation of God's love for us,
    that God sent his only Son into the world
    that we might have life through him.
Love consists in this:
    it is not we who loved God,
    but God loved us and sent his Son
    to expiate our sins.
My dear friends,
    if God loved us so much,
    we too should love each other.

Respect the elders and love the young.

No one has ever seen God,
    but as long as we love each other
    God remains in us
    and his love comes to its perfection in us.

Our Father... Hail Mary...

Concluding Prayer

Inspire, Lord,
all our actions and sustain them to the end,
so that all our prayer and work may begin with you,
and be brought by you to completion.
Through Christ our Lord. Amen.

Pray for your enemies out of love for Christ.

THURSDAY

Prayer of Thanksgiving

May the thanks we express this evening, Lord,
be for us a foretaste of the grateful joy
which will fill our hearts when your kingdom comes.
Until then, let us grow ever stronger
in faith, hope and love.
Through Christ our Lord. Amen.

Psalm 61

In God alone is my soul at rest;
my help comes from him.
He alone is my rock, my stronghold,
my fortress: I stand firm.

In God alone be at rest, my soul;
for my hope comes from him.
He alone is my rock, my stronghold,
my fortress: I stand firm.

In God is my safety and glory,
the rock of my strength.
Take refuge in God all you people.
Trust him at all times.
Pour out your hearts before him
for God is our refuge.

If you have a dispute with someone, make peace with him
before the sun goes down.

For God has said only one thing:
only two do I know:
that to God alone belongs power
and to you, Lord, love;
and that you repay each man
according to his deeds.

Reading   *Philippians 2: 3- 11*

Nothing is to be done out of jealousy or vanity;
    instead, out of humility of mind
      everyone should give preference to others,
      everyone pursuing not selfish interests,
      but those of others.
Make your own the mind of Christ Jesus:
Who being in the form of God
    did not count equality with God
    something to be grasped.
    But he emptied himself
    taking the form of a slave,
and being in every way like a human being,
    he was humbler yet,
    even to accepting death,
    death on a cross.

Never lose hope in God's mercy.

And for this God raised him high,
    and gave him the name
    which is above all other names,
    so that all beings
    in the heavens, on earth and in the underworld,
    should bend the knee at the name of Jesus
    and that every tongue should acclaim
    Jesus Christ as Lord,
    to the glory of God the Father.

Our Father... Hail Mary...

Concluding Prayer

I hand over to your care, Lord,
my soul and body, my mind and thoughts,
my prayers and my hopes, my health and my work,
my life and my death, my parents and my family,
my friends and my neighbours,
my country and all men.
Today and always. Amen.

The first step of humility is unhesitating obedience.

FRIDAY

Prayer of Thanksgiving

Thank you, heavenly Father,
for the graces you have given us today.
Thank you for inviting us
to share in the sufferings of your Son
and so to follow him, to glory.
By your Holy Spirit,
give us strength and encouragement this evening,
and let us love one another.
Through Christ our Lord. Amen.

Psalm 85

Turn your ear, O Lord, and give answer
for I am poor and needy.
Preserve my life, for I am faithful:
save the servant who trusts in you.

You are my God, have mercy on me, Lord,
for I cry to you all the day long.
Give joy to your servant, O Lord,
for to you I lift up my soul.

O Lord, you are good and forgiving,
full of love to all who call.
Give heed, O Lord, to my prayer
and attend to the sound of my voice.

It is love that impels them to pursue everlasting life.

I will praise you, Lord my God, with all my heart
and glorify your name for ever;
for your love to me has been great;
you have saved me from the depths of the grave.

Reading   *1 Cor 13: 1-8*

Though I command languages
    both human and angelic - if I speak without love,
    I am no more than a gong booming
    or a cymbal clashing.
And though I have the power of prophecy,
    to penetrate all mysteries and knowledge,
    and though I have all the faith
    necessary to move mountains -
    if I am without love, I am nothing.
Though I should give away to the poor
    all that I possess,
    and even give up my body to be burned -
    if I am without love,
    it will do me no good whatever.
Love is always patient and kind;
    love is never jealous;
    love is not boastful or conceited,
    it is never rude,
    and never seeks its own advantage,
    it does not take offence or store up grievances.

The disciples' obedience must be given gladly.

Love does not rejoice at wrongdoing,
> but finds joy in the truth.
It is always ready to make allowances,
> to trust, to hope, and to endure whatever comes.
Love never comes to an end.

> *Our Father... Hail Mary...*

Concluding Prayer
Father,
you made us in your own image
and your Son accepted death for our salvation.
Help us to keep watch in prayer at all times.
May we be free from sin when we leave this world
and rejoice in your peace for ever. Amen.

There are times when good words are to be left unsaid out of esteem for silence.

SATURDAY

Prayer of Thanksgiving

Accept our thanks, Lord God,
for the many wonders and gifts you have lavished on us.
Teach us this evening to look forward with joy
to when we shall offer you our praise
in union with Mary and all the saints
in the glory of your kingdom.
Through Christ our Lord. Amen.

Psalm 129

Out of the depths I cry to you, O Lord,
Lord, hear my voice!
O let your ears be attentive
to the voice of my pleading.

If you, O Lord, should mark our guilt,
Lord, who would survive?
But with you is found forgiveness:
for this we revere you.

My soul is waiting for the Lord,
I count on his word.
My soul is longing for the Lord
more than the watchman for daybreak.
(Let the watchman count on daybreak
and Israel on the Lord.)

Speaking and teaching are the master's task; the disciple is to be silent and listen.

Because with the Lord there is mercy
and fullness of redemption.
Israel indeed he will redeem
from all its iniquity.

Reading   Romans 8: 31-32,35,37-39

If God is for us, who can be against us?
Since he did not spare his own Son,
    but gave him up for the sake of all of us,
    then can we not expect
    that with him he will freely give us all his gifts?
Can anything cut us off from the love of Christ -
    can hardships or distress,
    or persecution,
    or lack of food and clothing,
    or threats or violence?
No, we come through all these things
    triumphantly victorious,
    by the power of him who loved us.
For I am certain of this:
    neither death nor life,
    nor angels, nor principalities,
    nothing already in existence
    and nothing still to come,
    nor any power,
    nor the heights nor the depths,

We absolutely condemn in all places any vulgarity and gossip.

nor any created thing whatever,
will be able to come between us
and the love of God,
known to us in Christ Jesus our Lord.

Our Father... Hail Mary...

Concluding Prayer

Remember, O most loving Virgin Mary,
that it is a thing unheard of,
that anyone fled to your protection,
implored your help, or sought your intercession
and was left forsaken.
Filled, therefore, with confidence in your goodness,
I fly to you, O Mother, Virgin of virgins,
to you do I come, before you I stand,
a sorrowful sinner.
Despise not my words, O Mother of the Word,
but graciously hear and grant my prayer. Amen.

We descend by exaltation and ascend by humility.

NIGHT PRAYER

In the name of the Father, and of the Son and of the
Holy Spirit. Amen.

Almighty Father, before we sleep, give us your
blessing and forgiveness.

*It is customary at the end of the day to make an examination of
conscience (see page 102) and to make an Act of Contrition:*

Lord, accept our sorrow for our sins,
forgive us for our faults of thought and word,
for what we have done,
and for what we have failed to do.
Restore us to the likeness of your Son,
and grant us that peace which the world cannot give.
Through Christ our Lord. Amen.

Psalm 4

When I call, answer me, O God of Justice;
from anguish you released me, have mercy and hear me!
O men, how long will your hearts be closed,
will you love what is futile and seek what is false?

It is the Lord who grants favours
    to those whom he loves;
the Lord hears me whenever I call him.
Fear him, do not sin:
ponder on your bed and be still.

If we humble our hearts the Lord will raise them to heaven.

Make justice your sacrifice
and trust in the Lord.
"What can bring us happiness?" many say.
Lift up the light of your face on us, O Lord.

You have put into my heart a greater joy
than they have from abundance of corn and new wine.
I will lie down in peace and sleep comes at once
for you alone, Lord, make me dwell in safety.

Reading

1 Peter 1: 3-5

Blessed be God, the Father of Our Lord Jesus Christ,
    who in his great mercy
      has given us a new birth into a living hope
      through the resurrection of Jesus Christ
      from the dead, and into a heritage
      that can never be spoilt or soiled
      and never fade away.
It is reserved in heaven for you who are being kept safe
      by God's power through faith
      until the salvation which has been prepared
      is revealed at the final point of time.

The Nunc Dimittis

Antiphon: Save us Lord, while we are awake;
         protect us while we sleep,
         that we may keep watch with Christ
         and rest with him in peace.

---

*The first step of humility is that a man keeps the fear of God
always before his eyes.*

Now Lord you have kept your word;
let your servant go in peace.

With my own eyes I have seen the salvation
which you have prepared in the sight of every people -

a light to reveal you to the nations
and the glory of your people Israel.

Glory be to the Father, etc.

Antiphon: Save us Lord, while we are awake; etc.

Concluding prayer

Visit, we pray you Lord, this house and family,
and drive far from it all the snares of the enemy.
Let your holy angels dwell in this place
for our protection and peace,
and let your blessing be always upon us.
Through Christ our Lord. Amen.

Blessing

May the Lord grant us peace this night, and perfect
peace hereafter.

*(Traditionally, night prayer ends with one of the antiphons
to Our Lady(see pages 150-3)).*

---

*He must constantly remember everything God has
commanded.*

PRAYING THE SCRIPTURES

The words of Sacred Scripture are words of God. They come down to us written by human hand, but are inspired by the Holy Spirit. Each page of every book of the Bible is an invitation to listen to the voice of our Creator. "In the sacred books the Father who is in heaven comes lovingly to meet his children and talks with them" (Vat II - Dei Verbum, ch 6, para 21). To open the Bible or a prayer book with passages from Scripture, to listen to the Sacred Text being proclaimed in a public liturgy is a moment of encounter with the God in whom "we live, and move, and exist" (Acts 17: 28), "who created my inmost self, knit me together in my mother's womb" (Psalm 139) and so passionately wants us to love and know Him.

Sometimes when we read Scripture, a word, a phrase or sentence strikes us in some way. It might be the mood of a Psalm, the manner in which a person acts or talks in the Old or New Testament, a saying, an expression of a prophet, of an apostle or of Christ himself in the Gospels. Something illumines us inside. When this occurs a very special thing is happening: God is talking to our heart, telling us something important for our life here and now. We should treasure what is being said to us, take the message

All who fear God have everlasting life awaiting them.

away with us, keep repeating it to ourselves at other times during the day if we haven't got the time to let it sink in right there and then. The text may be addressing a problem at work, in the family or a particular situation in a relationship. It may seem to give us the words we have been trying to find to express an emotion of joy, of sadness, frustration or mere contentment. The Word may seem to be answering a really profound question that we have been asking for some time or simply give us the indefinable sense that God is very close, very present in our life. Indeed, in these moments we can experience how God's Word is "a power that is working among us" (1 Thess 2: 13). For "the Word of God is something alive and active: it cuts more incisively than any two-edged sword. No created thing is hidden from him; everything is uncovered and stretched fully open" (Heb 4: 12-13).

It doesn't just stop there. Scripture is not simply a matter of letting God tell us things. We must feel free to respond to him in prayer, "so that a dialogue takes place between God and man. For, 'we speak to him when we pray: we listen to him when we read the Divine Oracles' (St Ambrose)" (Vat II - Dei Verbum ch 6, para 25). Scripture stirs us up deep down. It is the food of prayer. Indeed, it was the expressed wish of

---

His actions everywhere are in God's sight and are reported by angels at every hour.

Pope Paul VI that Sacred Scriptures should become "the principal source of all Christian prayer". For God's Word enters our heart if only we will let it, and there it kindles the sparks of the spirit that dwell there through our Baptism. There we are provoked by the Word to respond to Him. We can be filled with thanksgiving, with repentance, a desire to ask for things when we feel touched by God's Word or simply feel drawn to the prayer of attentive silence, a resting in the intangible presence of the Lord.

At other times we may feel nothing when we read or listen to Scripture. The words can seem unintelligible, distant, awkward, dry, offensive even. This should not worry us. We should try to continue to keep ourselves regularly in the Word of God through the downs as much as the ups, through all those moments of confusion, of depression, tiredness, apathy. For a piece of Scripture that means nothing to us one day can come to mind another in a new light. "For, as the rain and the snow come down from the sky and do not return before having watered the earth, fertilising it and making it germinate to provide seed for the sower and food to eat, so it is with the word that goes from my mouth: it will not return to me unfulfilled or before having carried out my good pleasure and having achieved what it was sent to do." (Is 55: 10)

We must be on guard against any base desire, because death is stationed near the gateway of pleasure.

PRAYING THE SCRIPTURES

Saint Benedict made the voice of God in Sacred Scripture the focus of his monk's day in the Divine Office and Lectio Divina. We too can live in this spirit by bringing a variety of different psalms and other passages from the Bible into the pattern of our daily lives. In this way "Let us, then, open our eyes to the divine light, and hear with our ears the divine voice as it cries out to us daily. 'Today if you hear his voice harden not your hearts', and again, 'He who has ears to hear, let him hear what the Spirit says to the Churches'." (Prol. RSB v 9–12)

The second step of humility is that a man loves not his own will.

THE HOLY EUCHARIST

This is the centre of our lives as Christians. In it we are united with Christ crucified and risen, through Him we are enabled to offer perfect worship to the Father, and we receive from Him light and strength to live our lives as they should be led. The Eucharist is the greatest and most important act we can perform in this life.

We begin by listening to God's Word in the Scriptures. These remind us of the immensity of His love for us, of the great deeds he has done for us, and the great gifts He has given us. We learn that His love will never fail, despite our frequent backslidings.

If we listen carefully and attentively we shall find guidance here on how best to live in the situation in which we find ourselves. This is especially true of the Gospel reading, in which through Jesus the Father speaks most clearly and directly to us.

The homily which follows helps us to focus on the aspects of God's message which affect us particularly in our present time and place.

In the Creed we re-affirm our faith and our trust in Him, and we go on to pray for our own needs, the needs of the Church and of the whole world. This is the beginning of the response we make to what we know God has done for us.

The Offertory continues this response. The bread and wine symbolise the offering we are making of ourselves, our work, our relationships, our world, our whole lives - we are offering all this to God to be healed and remade through the Death and Resurrection present to us here and now, to unite our own offering with that most perfect offering. This is done in the Eucharistic Prayer. It is the deepest and holiest part of the Eucharist , which carries us into the heart of God, to share His inner life.

When we hear the Preface and sing the angelic hymn, "Holy, Holy" we should forget our trivial and selfish preoccupations, and prepare to plunge into the mystery of Christ crucified and risen, which we recall and represent in the Eucharistic Prayer, especially at the consecration of the bread and wine in the words spoken by Jesus at the Last Supper: "This is my Body ...This is my Blood." The bread and wine are thus transformed into the body and blood of Christ.

In all of this we are not just making our own personal prayer; we are caught up in Christ's prayer as He pleads eternally to the Father for the whole human race and the whole world throughout history. We drop into that and let it carry us where God wants us to go.

United with Christ in this way, we go on to pray to the Father in the words Jesus gave us Himself, praying with Him and in Him.

The Communion follows in which God gives himself to us again as He did through the Scripture readings, but this time in a much deeper and more intimate way. We eat the flesh of Christ and drink His blood, under the appearance of bread and wine, which brings us peace and union. Our loneliness and disunity are overcome; we are one with God and one with each other, a single community and a single body, united with all the Christians who have ever been and who ever will be. We should try at this point to be still and quiet, letting the presence of God sink into us and transform us.

The final prayer and blessing send us out into the world again, strengthened, illumined, and ready to serve God in whatever way He calls us. It is a good practice when the Eucharist is over to remain in the Church for a little while in silent prayer, giving thanks for what we have shared in and pondering on its meaning. There is no more perfect spiritual act that we can perform than the Eucharist. We should be immensely grateful that it has been given to us, and make as frequent use of it as we can.

PRAYERS AFTER COMMUNION

Adoro te devote

Adoro te devote, latens Deitas,
Quae sub his figuris vere latitas;
Tibi se cor meum totum subjicit
Quia te contemplans totum deficit.

Visus, tactus, gustus in te fallitur,
Sed auditu solo tuto creditur.
Credo quidquid dixit Dei Filius:
Nil hoc verbo Veritatis verius.

In cruce latebat sola Deitas,
At hic latet simul et Humanitas;
Ambo tamen credens atque confitens,
Peto quod petivit latro paenitens.

Plagas, sicut Thomas, non intueor,
Deum tamen meum te confiteor.
Fac me tibi semper magis credere,
In te spem habere, te diligere.

O memoriale mortis Domini,
Panis vivus vitam prasestans homini!
Praesta meae menti de te vivere,
Et te illi semper dulce sapere.

Pie pelicane Jesu Domine,
Me immundum munda tuo sanguine,
Cujus una stilla salvum facere
Totum mundum quit ab omni scelere.

Adoro te devote

Hidden God, devoutly I adore Thee
Truly present underneath these veils.
All my heart subsides itself before Thee
Since it all before Thee faints and fails.

Not to sight or taste or touch be credit;
Hearing only do we trust secure.
I believe, for God the Son has said it,
Word of Truth that ever shall endure.

On the Cross was veiled Thy Godhead's splendour;
Here thy Manhood lieth hidden too.
Unto both alike my faith I render
And, as sued the contrite thief, I sue.

Though I look not on Thy wounds, with Thomas
Thee my Lord and Thee my God I call.
Make me more and more believe Thy promise,
Hope in Thee and love Thee over all.

O memorial of my Saviour dying,
Living Bread, that givest life to man,
May my soul its life from Thee supplying
Taste Thy sweetness as on earth it can.

Deign, O Jesus, Pelican of Heaven,
Me a sinner in Thy blood to lave,
To a single drop of which is given
All the world from all its sin to save.

Jesu, quem velatum nunc aspicio,
Oro, fiat illud quod tam sitio:
Ut te revelata cernens facie
Visu sim beatus tuae gloriae.

attributed to Saint Thomas Aquinas (1225-1274)

Anima Christi

Anima Christi, sanctifica me.
Corpus Christi, salva me.
Sanguis Christi, inebria me.
Aqua lateris Christi, lava me.
Passio Christi, conforta me.
O bone Jesu, exaudi me.
Intra tua vulnera absconde me.
Ne permittas me separari a te.
Ab hoste maligno defende me.
In hora mortis meæ voca me,
Et jube me venire ad te,
Ut cum sanctis tuis laudem te
In sæcula sæculorum.
Amen.

Ave verum

Ave, verum Corpus, natum
De Maria Virgine;
Vere passum, immolatum
In cruce pro homine.

As I contemplate Thy hidden presence,
Grant me what I thirst for and implore:
In the revelation of Thine Essence
To behold Thy glory evermore.

Anima Christi

Soul of Christ, sanctify me.
Body of Christ, save me.
Blood of Christ, inebriate me.
Water from the side of Christ, wash me.
Passion of Christ, strengthen me.
O good Jesus, hear me.
Within Thy wounds hide me.
Suffer me not to be separated from thee.
From the malicious enemy defend me.
In the hour of my death call me,
And bid me come unto Thee.
That with Thy saints I may praise Thee.
For ever and ever.
Amen.

Ave verum

Hail to thee, true Body, sprung
From the Virgin Mary's womb,
The same that on the Cross was hung
And bore for man the bitter doom.

Cujus latus perforatum
Aqua fluxit et sanguine,
Esto nobis prægustatum
Mortis in examine.

O Jesu dulcis, O Jesu pie,
O Jesu, fili Mariæ.

O Salutaris

O salutaris hostia,
Quæ cæli pandis ostium,
Bella premunt hostilia;
Da robur, fer auxilium.

Uni trinoque Domino
Sit sempiterna gloria,
Qui vitam sine termino
Nobis donet in patria. Amen.

The fourth step of humility is that his heart quietly embraces suffering.

Thou whose side was pierced and flowed
Both with water and with blood
Suffer us to taste of Thee
In our life's last agony.

O kind, O loving One,
O sweet Jesus, Mary's Son.

O Salutaris

O saving victim, pledge of love,
Who openest heaven's gates above,
By hostile wars we are oppressed;
Be Thou our strength, support and rest.

To God the Father and the Son
And Holy Spirit, three in one,
Be endless praise: may He above
With life immortal crown our love. Amen.

---

*The sixth step of humility is that he is content with the lowest
and most menial treatment.*

Prayer before a crucifix

O Jesus, so good and gentle, see how I kneel before your image on the cross and beg of you most earnestly that you would give me in my heart the living imprint of faith, hope and charity with true repentance for my sins and a strong will to reform my life according to your will. As I ask you to grant me this I have the image of your five wounds before my eyes. I think of those wounds and reflect in my mind on their meaning and I am deeply moved to grief and sympathy for your great suffering; I remember the words of the Psalmist attributed to you: They have torn holes in my hands and my feet and have numbered all my bones.

Come, Lord, work upon us, set us on fire and clasp us close, be fragrant to us, draw us to your loveliness, let us love, let us run to you.

Saint Augustine (354-430)

Love of God

You who are love itself give me the grace of love, give me yourself, so that all my days may finally empty into the one day of your eternal life.

Karl Rahner (1904-1984)

The seventh step of humility is that a man is convinced in his heart that he is inferior to all.

The Divine Praises

Blessed be God.
Blessed be His Holy Name.
Blessed be Jesus Christ, true God and true Man.
Blessed be the Name of Jesus.
Blessed be His most Sacred Heart.
Blessed be His most precious Blood.
Blessed be Jesus in the most holy Sacrament
    of the Altar.
Blessed be the Holy Spirit, the Paraclete.
Blessed be the great Mother of God, Mary most holy.
Blessed be her holy and immaculate Conception.
Blessed be her glorious assumption.
Blessed be the name of Mary, Virgin and Mother.
Blessed be Saint Joseph, her Spouse most chaste.
Blessed be God in His angels and in His saints.

The ninth step of humility is that he controls his tongue.

PRAYING BEFORE THE BLESSED SACRAMENT

God is everywhere, so of course it is perfectly possible to pray to Him in any place and at any time. Nevertheless we find that in practice it is often easier to pray in a place where his presence is focused for us through Christ's sacramental presence in the Eucharist and by the rites and blessings of the Church. The Blessed Sacrament, reserved in the tabernacle, is an enormous help to prayer, and one which we ought to make frequent use of. It is natural that this should be so, since the Blessed Sacrament puts us in touch with the central mysteries of our religion - the mass, and the death and resurrection of Christ, from which flow all our spiritual knowledge and strength. So if we make a habit of dropping into a church or chapel each day to pray before the Blessed Sacrament, we shall find our spiritual lives enormously deepened and strengthened by it.

When we settle down to do this we should try to be as relaxed and natural as possible, since we are talking to our Father, and Jesus, His Son, is our friend and brother. At the same time we should have proper reverence and awe, remembering that God is also our creator and ruler of the universe. We can use one or

---

The eleventh step of humility is that he speaks gently.

several or all of the prayers on pp 90-95*, or if we like we can talk to God quite spontaneously in our own words. Sometimes we may prefer simply to be still and silent, relaxing in God's presence and listening for whatever He may have to say to us. In this way we shall build up a living relationship with Him which will strengthen us and guide us through our life.

*see also pp 108-130

All that he once performed with dread, he will now begin to observe out of love for Christ, good habit and delight in virtue.

THE SACRAMENT OF
RECONCILIATION

We are truly made children of God in baptism and member's of Christ's Body, which is the Church; but that is not the end of the story. It is a wonderful beginning of the new life which is Christ's gift to us, but in our hearts there is not only a new potential for love and good acts, which is given and confirmed through grace; there remains also the age-old threat of failure and wickedness, which arises from self-seeking and the temptations from which we are never free. It is inevitable, therefore, that from time to time out of weakness or ill-intent we will act or fail to act in a way that puts barriers between us and the God who loves us. That is what sin is. Whatever our own failure, however, God's love never fails and he always calls us back to repentance. His forgiveness, which is vividly illustrated in the Parable of the Prodigal Son (Lk 15: 11), is always available to us in the Sacrament of Reconciliation. Throughout our lives we need again and again to open our hearts to God's forgiveness for our failures large or small, just as the Prodigal Son turned to his father. That repentance leads us naturally to admit our faults in confession. Confession, in which we face ourselves truthfully, is itself therapeutic,

---

We believe that the divine presence is everywhere.

but the real healing and new grace and strength come from God's forgiveness. Christ is present in the sacrament. Through his Church and through the absolution pronounced in his name by the priest he gives us the grace and healing we need.

In preparing for this sacrament it may help if we begin by thanking God for his blessings this day, this week, this month. By doing this we are opening our eyes once again to the light of God's love for us. But as we do it we are bound to find that between us and the love of God there are things in ourselves that are getting in the way.

If you look at the setting sun, any obstacle in the way will appear as a black silhouette. If we look, thankfully and honestly, at God in prayer, things we have done or failed to do, things we have said, bitter feelings of grievance and resentment, will stand out quite clearly, getting in the way. These things are our sins. Sins are obstacles we put in the way of the love of God. Very serious sin will get so much in the way that its blackness can seem almost to blot out completely the light of God's love. But his love never fails, and it is because we know this that we are preparing for the sacrament of reconciliation.

Let us consider how we ought to behave in the presence of God and his angels.

If we find ourselves in darkness when we lift our eyes and hearts to God, and are not seeing the black shapes of our sins clearly enough to identify and describe them, which we must try to do in our confession, it may help to ask ourselves some questions. To see where our true faults lie we need God's help, so it is good to pray to the Holy Spirit in some such words as these:

Prayer to the Holy Spirit before Confession

Come, Holy Spirit, search my mind and heart. Help me to see clearly where I have gone wrong, to be truly sorry for it, and to confess it humbly and honestly. I ask this through Jesus Christ our Lord.

An Examination of Conscience

The following questions will help you examine your conscience. They are only guidelines; you may think of other questions which are more to the point in your case.

Is it too long since I last confessed?

Was my confession honest and did I do the penance given me?

Did I go to Communion without proper preparation or reverence?

Did I miss Mass on Sundays or Holy Days through my own fault?

Let us sing the psalms in such a way that our minds are in harmony with our voices.

RECONCILIATION

Am I wilfully distracted or irreverent during Mass, and do I disturb others?.

Do I pray regularly each morning and night, or do I sometimes forget or not bother?

Have I treated holy things with irreverence?

Am I proud or conceited? Do I despise some people?

Have I been ungenerous or stubborn?

Have I been unco-operative or ungrateful with people who are trying to help me, such as colleagues, family or teachers?

Have I been quarrelsome? or sulky? or jealous? or easily moved to anger?

Have I turned my back on someone who needed my help?

Have I failed to speak out against things I know to be wrong for fear of becoming unpopular?

Have I prevented justice being done?

Have I told lies to get out of trouble, to make myself seem better than I am?

Have I refused to apologise when I hurt someone?

Have I stolen things, or borrowed them without the owner's consent?

Have I said unpleasant or spiteful things about other people?

Have I bullied people, or used them to my own ends?

---

*God regards our purity of heart and tears of compunction,
not our many words.*

RECONCILIATION

Do I make friends with people because I like and respect them, or because they have power or influence or reputation?

Have I been deliberately cruel or malicious?

Have I led other people into wrongdoing?

Have I harboured impure thoughts or given way to them?

Have I had sex outside marriage, or committed adultery?

Do I eat or drink too much?

Finally, do God and other people mean anything to me, or do I live only for myself?

The confession itself should be made simply, and clearly without making excuses or holding anything back. Your confession is between you and God. The priest is God's representative to pronounce His forgiveness through the words of absolution in the name of the Church. He may also add a brief word of advice and encouragement.

Prayer should be short and pure unless perhaps it is prolonged under the inspiration of divine grace.

RECONCILIATION

Before the priest gives you absolution, he will invite you to make an Act of Contrition expressing your sorrow for what you have done, and promising to amend it, with God's grace, in the future. You can use some such words as these:

Acts of Contrition

i) O my God, because you are so good, I am very sorry that I have sinned against you, and with the help of your grace I will not sin again.

ii) Lord Jesus, you chose to be called the friend of sinners. By your saving death and resurrection free me from by sins. May your peace take root in my heart and bring forth a harvest of love, holiness, and truth.

iii) O my God, I am sorry and beg pardon for all my sins, and detest them above all things, because they deserve your dreadful punishments, because they have crucified my loving Saviour Jesus Christ, and, most of all, because they offend your infinite goodness; and I firmly resolve, by the help of your grace, never to offend you again, and carefully to avoid the occasions of sin.

Every age and level of understanding should receive appropriate treatment.

iv) God our Father, I thank you for loving me. I am sorry for all my sins, for what I have done and for what I have failed to do. I will sincerely try to love you and others in everything I do and say. Help me to walk in your light today and always.

v) O God, I am sorry for my unfaithfulness to the love you show me by the gift of life and the greater gift of union with you through the grace of baptism. I beg you to forgive my sins, heal the wounds they leave and strengthen me in my weakness. I thank you for your mercy which has drawn me to repentance and for the forgiveness you freely give me in the sacrament of reconciliation.

The priest will ask you to perform a penance - some prayer or religious act to show that you are truly sorry for the past and that you really want to do better from now on. The penance is best done as soon as possible after the confession. You may like to add to it this prayer for conversion and amendment.

A kind word is better than the best gift.

Prayer after Confession

Merciful Lord, with a pure heart I thank you for taking away my sins. Let your Holy Spirit guide my life so that my soul may bear the fruit of love, joy, peace, patience, kindness, goodness, trustfulness, gentleness and self-control. Renew my desire to be your faithful friend and servant, increase my loving dependence on you, and grant me that joy and peace of heart which comes from doing your holy will. Through Christ our Lord. Amen.

It is a good habit to go to confession regularly, even if you have not committed any very serious sins. There is a special grace of healing which comes from this sacrament and which helps build up our relationship with God even when we only have small things to confess. This sacrament is a great and powerful gift, and we should use it.

Whoever needs less should thank God and not be distressed.

PRAYERS TO KNOW BY HEART

The Lord's Prayer

Pater noster, qui es in cælis,
sanctificetur nomen tuum;
adveniat regnum tuum;
fiat voluntas tua, sicut in cælo, et in terra.
Panem nostrum quotidianum da nobis hodie;
et dimitte nobis debita nostra,
sicut et nos dimittimus debitoribus nostris;
et ne nos inducas in tentationem;
sed libera nos a malo. Amen.

The Hail Mary

Ave Maria, gratia plena;
Dominus tecum;
benedicta tu in mulieribus,
et benedictus fructus ventris tui Jesus.
Sancta Maria, Mater Dei,
ora pro nobis peccatoribus nunc,
et in hora mortis nostræ. Amen.

Whoever needs more should feel humble because of his weakness.

The Lord's Prayer

Our Father, who art in heaven,
hallowed be thy name;
thy kingdom come,
thy will be done on earth as it is in heaven.
Give us this day our daily bread;
and forgive us our trespasses,
as we forgive those that trespass against us;
and lead us not into temptation,
but deliver us from evil. Amen.

The Hail Mary

Hail Mary, full of grace,
the Lord is with thee.
Blessed art thou amongst women,
and blessed is the fruit of thy womb, Jesus.
Holy Mary, Mother of God,
pray for us sinners, now,
and at the hour of our death. Amen.

---

*There must be no word or sign of the evil of grumbling for
any reason at all.*

TRADITIONAL PRAYERS

The Doxology

Gloria Patri, et Filio,
et Spiritui Sancto.
Sicut erat in principio,
et nunc, et semper
et in sæcula sæculorum.
Amen.

Glory be to the Father
and to the Son
and to the Holy Spirit.
As it was in the
beginning,
is now and ever shall be
world without end.
Amen.

The Apostles' Creed

I believe in God, the Father almighty,
creator of heaven and earth,
and in Jesus Christ, his only Son, our Lord,
who was conceived by the Holy Spirit,
born of the Virgin Mary, suffered under Pontius
Pilate, was crucified, died, and was buried.
He descended into hell.
The third day he rose again from the dead.
He ascended into heaven,
and sitteth at the right hand of God the Father
almighty. From thence he shall come to judge
the living and the dead.
I believe in the Holy Spirit, the Holy Catholic Church,
the Communion of Saints, the forgiveness of sins,
the resurrection of the body, and life everlasting.
Amen.

The brothers should serve one another.

The Confiteor

I confess to almighty God, to blessed Mary, ever virgin, to blessed Michael the archangel, to blessed John the Baptist, to the holy apostles Peter and Paul, and to all the saints, that I have sinned exceedingly in thought, word and deed, through my fault, through my fault, through my most grievous fault. Therefore I beseech blessed Mary, ever virgin, blessed Michael the archangel, blessed John the Baptist, the holy apostles Peter and Paul, and all the saints to pray for me to the Lord our God.

May almighty God have mercy on us, forgive us our sins and bring us to life everlasting. Amen.

May the almighty and merciful Lord grant us pardon, absolution and remission of our sins. Amen.

Act of Contrition

O God, I am sorry for my unfaithfulness to the love you show me by the gift of life and the greater gift of union with you through the grace of baptism. I beg you to forgive my sins, heal the wounds they leave and strengthen me in my weakness. I thank you for your mercy which has drawn me to repentance and for the forgiveness you freely give me in the sacrament of reconciliation.

Service increases reward and fosters love.

I thank thee, Lord, for knowing me better than I know myself, and for letting me know myself better than others know me. Make me, I pray, better than they suppose, and forgive me for what they do not know. Lord Jesus, eternal word of the Father, who brought us the words of the gospel, grant me through them, to know you, and to know myself. Show me my wretchedness and your mercy; my sin and your grace; my poverty and your riches; my weakness and your strength; my stupidity and your wisdom; my darkness and your light.

The Jesus Prayer

Two men went up to the Temple to pray, one a Pharisee, the other a tax collector. The Pharisee stood there and said this prayer to himself: "I thank you, God, that I am not grasping, unjust, adulterous like the rest of mankind, and particularly that I am not like this tax collector here" ... The tax collector stood some distance away, not daring even to raise his eyes to heaven; but he beat his breast and said: "God, be merciful to me a sinner."

(Luke 18: 10)

Lord Jesus Christ, Son of God,
be merciful to me a sinner.

Let those who are not strong have help so that they may serve without distress.

PRAYERS OF THE SAINTS

Prayer of Saint Benedict

Actiones nostras quaesumus, Domine, aspirando praeveni et adiuvando prosequere ut cuncta nostra oratio et operatio a te semper incipiat et per te incepta finiatur.

We pray, Lord, that everything we do may be prompted by your inspiration, so that every prayer and work of ours may begin from you and be brought by you to completion.

Prayer based on the Prologue of Saint Benedict's Rule

Almighty God, who has given us grace at this time with one accord to make our common supplications to you and promised that when two or three are gathered together in your name you will grant their requests: fulfil now, O Lord, the desires and petitions of your servants, as may be most expedient for them, granting us in this world knowledge of your truth, and in the world to come life everlasting.

Saint John Chrysostom (349-407)

Care of the sick must rank above and before all else, so that they may truly be served as Christ.

For behold you were within me, and I outside;
and I sought you outside and in my ugliness fell upon
those lovely things that you have made.
You were with me and I was not with you.
I was kept from you by those things,
yet had they not been in you,
they would not have been at all.
You called and cried to me
and broke upon my deafness;
and you sent forth your light and shone upon me,
and chased away my blindness.
You breathed fragrance upon me,
and I drew in my breath and do now pant for you;
you touched me, and I have burned for your peace.

Saint Augustine (354-430)

Give me, O Lord, a steadfast heart which no
unworthy thought can drag downwards; an
unconquered heart which no tribulation can wear out;
an upright heart which no unworthy purpose may
tempt aside. Give me also, O Lord my God,
understanding to know you, diligence to seek you,
wisdom to find you, and a faithfulness that may
finally embrace you through Jesus Christ, our Lord.

Saint Thomas Aquinas (1225-1274)

---

*Nothing is so inconsistent with the life of any Christian as
overindulgence.*

Give us, Lord, a humble, quiet, peaceable, patient, tender and charitable mind, and in all our thoughts, words and deeds a taste of the Holy Spirit. Give us, Lord, a lively faith, a firm hope, a fervent charity, a love of you. Take from us all lukewarmness in meditation, dullness in prayer. Give us fervour and delight in thinking of you and your grace, your tender compassion towards us. The things that we pray for, good Lord, give us grace to labour for; through Jesus Christ our Lord.

Saint Thomas More (1477-1535)

God, our Father, we are exceedingly frail and indisposed to every virtuous and gallant undertaking. Strengthen our weakness, we beseech you, that we may do valiantly in this spiritual war; help us against our own negligence and cowardice, and defend us from the treachery of our unfaithful hearts; for Jesus Christ's sake.

Thomas à Kempis (1380-1471)

Nothing is to be preferred to the Work of God.

Let me love myself only if I love thee,
And do all things for thy sake.
Let me humble myself and exalt thee,
And think of nothing else but thee.
Let me die to myself and live in thee,
And take whatever happens as coming from thee.
Let me forsake myself and walk after thee,
And ever desire to follow thee.
Let me flee from myself and turn to thee,
That so I may merit to be defended by thee.
Let me fear for myself, let me fear thee,
And be among those that are chosen by thee.
Let me distrust myself and trust in thee,
And ever obey for the love of thee.
Let me cleave to nothing but thee,
And ever be poor because of thee.
Look upon me that I may love thee.
Call me, that I may see thee,
And forever possess thee, for all eternity.

Saint Augustine (354-430)

Idleness is the enemy of the soul.

Lord, make me an instrument of your peace; where there is hatred let me sow peace, where there is injury let me sow pardon, where there is doubt let me sow faith, where there is despair let me give hope, where there is darkness let me give light, where there is sadness let me give joy. O Divine Master, grant that I may not try to be comforted but to comfort, not try to be understood but to understand, not try to be loved but to love. Because it is in giving that we receive, it is in forgiving that we are forgiven, and it is in dying that we are born to eternal life.

Saint Francis of Assisi (1182-1226)

O Jesus, watch over me always, especially today, or I shall betray you like Judas.

Saint Philip Neri (1515-1595)

All things are to be done with moderation on account of the fainthearted.

Searching for God

O Lord my God,
Teach my heart this day where and how to see you,
where and how to find you.
You have made me and remade me,
and you have bestowed on me
all the good things I possess,
and still I do not know you.
I have not yet done that for which I was made.
Teach me to seek you,
for I cannot seek you unless you teach me,
or find you unless you show yourself to me.
Let me seek you in my desire,
let me desire you in my seeking.
Let me find you by loving you,
let me love you when I find you.

Saint Anselm (1033-1109)

Self Offering

Take, Lord, all my liberty. Receive my memory, my understanding, and my whole will. Whatever I have and possess, you have given to me; to you I restore it wholly, and to your will I utterly surrender it for my direction. Give me the love of you only, with your grace, and I am rich enough; nor do I ask anything besides.

Saint Ignatius Loyola (1491-1556)

All guests who present themselves are to be welcomed as Christ.

118

Thanks be to you, my Lord Jesus Christ, for all the benefits and blessings which you have given to me, for all the pains and insults which you have borne for me. O most merciful Friend, Brother and Redeemer, may I know you more clearly, love you more dearly, and follow you more nearly.

Saint Richard of Chichester (1198-1253)

Watch, dear Lord with those who wake or watch or weep tonight, and give your angels charge over those who sleep. Tend your sick ones, O Lord Jesus Christ, rest your weary ones, bless your dying ones, soothe your suffering ones, shield your joyous ones, and all for your love's sake.

attributed to Saint Augustine (354-430)

The Grace

The Grace of Our Lord Jesus Christ, the love of God and the fellowship of the Holy Spirit be with us all.

Saint Paul (Gal, 13)

Proper honour must be shown to all, especially to those who share our faith.

PRAYERS FOR VARIOUS NEEDS

Prayers before Study

Come, O Holy Spirit, fill the hearts of your faithful and bring to life in them the fire of your love. Send forth your spirit; they are created, and you renew the face of the earth.

Let us pray
O God, who first taught the faithful in their hearts by the light of the Holy Spirit, grant that by receiving the same gift of the Spirit we may be truly wise and always rejoice in his consolation. Through Christ our Lord. Amen.

    Hail Mary etc.
    St Benedict and St Lawrence, pray for us.

Prayer to the Holy Spirit

Father, pour out your Spirit upon your people,
and grant us a new vision of your glory,
a new experience of your power,
a new faithfulness to your Word,
and a new consecration to your service,
that your love may grow among us,
and your kingdom come;
Through Christ our Lord. Amen.

Great care and concern are to be shown in receiving poor people, because in them more particularly Christ is received.

God be in My Head

God be in my head, and in my understanding;
God be in my eyes, and in my looking;
God be in my mouth, and in my speaking;
God be in my heart, and in my thinking;
God be at mine end, and at my departing.

(from the Sarum rite)

God grant me the serenity
to accept the things I cannot change,
courage to change the things I can,
and wisdom to know the difference.

Reinhold Niebuhr

Alcuin's Prayer in the Night

He lay with quiet heart in the stern asleep;
waking, commanded both the winds and sea.
Christ, though this weary body slumber deep,
Grant that my heart may keep its watch with thee.
O Lamb of God that carried all our sin,
Guard thou my sleep against the enemy.

God's Presence In My World

Help me today to realise that you will be speaking to me
through the events of the day, through people,
through things, and through creation.
Give me ears, eyes and heart to perceive you,
however veiled your presence may be.

---

*The concern must be whether he truly seeks God and whether he
shows eagerness for the Work of God, for obedience and for trials.*

Give me insight to see through the exterior of things
to the interior truth.
Give me your Spirit of discernment.
O Lord, you know how busy I must be this day.
If I forget you, do not forget me.

Jacob Astley (1579-1652)

Saint Patrick's Breastplate
Prayer for Divine Assistance

*This is a modern version of a prayer found in an eleventh
century Life of St Patrick. St Patrick came from Britain, was
apostle of Ireland in the fifth century, but whether or not he
was original author of this prayer cannot be established.*

I arise today
in power and might.
I call upon the Trinity
with faith in the threeness
and trust in the oneness
of the great world's maker.

I arise today
in the power and might
of Christ's birth and baptism,
His crucifixion and burial,
His resurrection and ascension,
His coming anew to judge mankind.

This is the law under which you are choosing to serve.

TRADITIONAL PRAYERS

I arise today in love of cherubim,
in duty of angels,
in fealty of archangels,
in hope of uprising,
to gain Christ's reward.

I set my trust
in prayers of patriarchs,
in foretelling of prophets,
in preaching of apostles,
in witness of martyrs,
in faith of confessors,
in purity of virgins,
in good works of the just.

I arise today
with the powers of heaven,
the sun in brightness,
the moon in splendour,
the flashing of fire,
the swift stroke of lightning
the rushing of storm-wind,
the deepness of ocean,
the firmness of earth
the hardness of bed-rock.

---

*The younger ones must respect their seniors, and the seniors
must love their juniors .*

Christ save me today
from bane and from burning,
from drowning, from wounding
that grace abounding
may be my portion.

Christ be with me,
Christ within me,
Christ in my headway,
Christ in my wake,
Christ alow and Christ aloft,
Christ at my right hand,
Christ on my left,
Christ with me waking,
walking and sleeping.

Christ in every heart thinks on me,
Christ in every tongue speaks to me,
Christ in every eye beholding,
Christ in every listening ear.

attributed to St Patrick (c. 390-460)

He must be chaste, temperate and merciful.

In God's Service

Lord God, whose we are and whom we serve,
help us to glorify you this day,
in all the thoughts of our hearts,
in all the words of our lips,
and in all the works of our hands,
as becomes those who are your servants,
through Jesus Christ our Lord.

Prayer of Dedication

Lord Jesus, I give you my hands to do your work, I
give you my feet to go your way. I give you my
tongue to speak your words. I give you my mind that
you may think in me. I give you my spirit that you
may pray in me. Above all I give you my heart that
you may love in me your Father, and all mankind. I
give you my whole self that you may grow in me, so
that it is you, Lord Jesus, who live and work and pray
in me.

---

*He should always let mercy triumph over judgment so that he
too may win mercy.*

A Prayer for Priests

Lord Jesus, you have chosen your priests from among us and sent them out to proclaim your word and to act in your name. For so great a gift to your Church, we give you praise and thanksgiving. We ask you to fill them with the fire of your love, that their ministry may reveal your presence in the Church. Since they are earthen vessels, we pray that your power shine through their weakness. In their afflictions let them never be crushed; in their doubts never despair; in temptation never be destroyed; in persecution never abandoned. Inspire them through prayer to live each day the mystery of your dying and rising. In times of weakness send them your Spirit, and help them to praise your heavenly father and pray for poor sinners. By the same Holy Spirit put your word on their lips and your love in their hearts, to bring good news to the poor and healing to the broken-hearted. And may the gift of Mary your mother, to the disciple whom you loved, be your gift to every priest. Grant that she who formed you in her human image, may form them in your divine image, by the power of your Spirit, to the glory of God the Father. Amen.

He must hate faults but love the brothers.

A Prayer for Monastic Vocations

It is in the silence of our hearts, O Lord,
that your voice calls us gently to turn from self-will
and surrender to you in our monastic vocation.
We thank you for that hidden gift
and pray that many others
may hear your call to monastic life.
May your loving grace give us strength
to persevere in St Benedict's way of peace
and to witness faithfully to the truth
and love of your Kingdom.
We ask this through Christ our Lord.

Grant, Lord, that those whom you call
to enter priesthood or religious life
may have the generosity to answer your call,
so that those who need your help may always find it.
We ask this through Christ our Lord. Amen.

In the Service of Others

Make us worthy, Lord, to serve our fellow men
throughout the world who live and die in poverty and
hunger. Give them through our hands this day their
daily bread, and by our understanding love, give
peace and joy.

Mother Teresa of Calcutta

Let him strive to be loved rather than feared.

May he support us all the day long, till the shades lengthen and the evening comes, and the busy world is hushed and the fever of life is over and our work is done. Then in his mercy may he give us a safe lodging and a holy rest and peace at the last.

Cardinal John Henry Newman (1801-1890)

A Prayer for Peace

O God, Creator of the universe who extends your paternal concern over every creature and guides the events of history to the goal of salvation, we acknowledge your fatherly love when you break the resistance of mankind and, in a world torn by strife and discord, you make us ready for reconciliation.

Renew for us the wonders of your mercy; send forth your Spirit that he may work in the intimacy of hearts, that enemies may begin to dialogue, that adversaries may shake hands and peoples may encounter one another in harmony.

May all commit themselves to the sincere search for true peace which will extinguish all arguments, for charity which overcomes hatred, for pardon which disarms revenge.

Pope John Paul II

Excitable, anxious, extreme, obstinate, jealous or oversuspicious he must not be. Such a man is never at rest.

PRAYERS TO SAINTS

Prayer for the intercession of Martyrs
O God our Father, whose gift of unflinching faith turns our native weakness into strength, help us to follow faithfully the example of the martyrs of these islands; and with the support of their prayers may we share their union with Christ in his Passion and Resurrection and so join them in eternal happiness. We ask this through Christ Our Lord.

Prayer to the Benedictine Saints of England

We pray to you, Saint Augustine of Canterbury,
and to all the Benedictine monks and nuns
whose prayer in this land through the centuries
left in so many ways and in so many places
the mark of God's presence
and the memory of holiness.
May their example inspire us
to stronger faith and deeper prayer,
and may their intercession
help us to be faithful in seeking God alone,
so that our witness may lead men and women to Him
even where He is most neglected and denied.

Trusting in God's help, he must in love obey.

Prayer to Saint Alban Roe

We pray to you, Saint Alban Roe,
for you were strong in faith
and cheerful in self-giving.
Remember before God your own community
and all they seek to help on the way to God.
Inspire us all to be generous like you
in the service of God and others
and to follow your example
of unwavering faith
in Christ Our Lord.

Prayer for Protection to Saint Michael

Holy Michael, Archangel,
defend us in the day of battle;
be our safeguard against the wickedness
and snares of the devil.
May God rebuke him, we humbly pray;
and do thou, prince of the heavenly host,
by the power of God thrust down to hell Satan,
and all wicked spirits who wander through the world
for the ruin of souls. Amen.

---

*Obedience is a blessing to be shown by all, not only to the
abbot but also to one another.*

THE STATIONS OF THE CROSS

I	Jesus is condemned to death
II	Jesus carries (takes up) his Cross
III	Jesus falls the first time
IV	Jesus meets his mother
V	Simon of Cyrene helps Jesus to carry his Cross
VI	Veronica wipes the face of Jesus
VII	Jesus falls the second time
VIII	Women of Jerusalem mourn for Jesus
IX	Jesus falls the third time
X	Jesus is stripped of his clothes
XI	Jesus is nailed to the Cross
XII	Jesus dies on the Cross
XIII	Jesus is taken down from the Cross and laid in his mother's arms
XIV	Jesus is placed in the tomb

It is by the way of obedience that we go to God.

Jesus died during a pilgrimage. Like countless Jews before and since, he had gone to celebrate the passover in Jerusalem. The closing stages of that pilgrimage are recalled in the Stations of the Cross, leading through his final hours. They are often made by a group walking from station to station, each scene depicted in a picture or even by large statues in a church or outside in the open air. But even an individual on his own meditating on the stations is conscious of them as a journey which he must make his own, a journey through suffering to death and beyond to Resurrection.

Consider some of the other people in the Journey with Jesus. Pilate, the unjust and cowardly judge; how often we set ourselves up in judgement of others. The soldiers, who torture, strip and crucify Jesus with professional indifference; how little do we reflect on the pain we cause others by our many unkind acts. Simon of Cyrene, reluctantly carrying the cross with Jesus; how unwilling we often are to shoulder the burdens of others. Veronica, whose small loving act of generosity imprints the face of Jesus on her towel; how we are imprinted with the image of Jesus through love. The women of Jerusalem, whose tears must be shed not for Jesus but for their children; how the sufferings of Christ should lead us towards

---

There is a good zeal which separates from evil and leads to God and everlasting life.

concern for the sufferings of people today and the real dangers facing the world. And finally Mary his Mother; receiving her dead son in her arms just as she had cradled the new-born infant, understanding all the sense of loss and misery of the widow who sees her own child die. The women in the story make the journey with love and courage. They stand at the foot of the Cross united with the suffering Christ and they lay him in his grave. It will be the women who will be the first witnesses of the Resurrection. Only through sharing in the pilgrimage through suffering can they come through death to the new life of glory.

No one is to pursue what he judges better for himself, but instead, what he judges better for someone else.

THE ROSARY

Why is the Rosary such a powerful prayer, and why has the Church down the ages so strongly recommended its use?

We should never think of Christ's birth, death and resurrection simply as historical events which happened a long time ago. If we ponder on them, soak our minds and hearts in them, they become present to us now, bringing us closer to God, changing our lives, making us more like what we should be.

The repeated prayers help to quieten our minds and to drive away distractions. We don't need to concentrate on the meaning of the words - in fact it is best not to, but simply to let them flow easily and naturally under the inspiration of the Holy Spirit, while we fix our minds on each Mystery in turn. Some people build up a clear mental picture of the events in each Mystery, but that doesn't suit everyone, and others find it more helpful simply to feel the events as strongly present, without trying to picture them in detail.

Let them prefer nothing whatever to Christ.

THE ROSARY

If you pray the Rosary frequently, you will probably find that after a while it develops a movement and a rhythm of its own, so that it becomes like a flowing stream, and all you have to do is let it carry you. That is because the Holy Spirit is praying with you and in you, drawing you into the heart of God. Our Lady is also praying with you. She was the first to witness these Mysteries and ponder on them in her heart; she is helping you to tune into them and grasp their meaning.

The more we pray the Rosary, the closer we shall draw to God, understand the Mysteries of Christ, and in the light of these understand the meaning of our own lives.

What page, what passage of the inspired books of the Old and New Testaments is not the truest of guides for human life?

THE FIVE JOYFUL MYSTERIES

1. The Annunciation

When the archangel Gabriel invites Mary to be the mother of the Messiah, she responds with faith and obedience.

> "Rejoice, you who enjoy God's favour! The Lord is with you. Look! You are to conceive and bear a son, and you must name him Jesus."

Luke 1: 28, 30, 31

2. The Visitation

Mary, full of the good news given to her, hurries to offer help and encouragement to Elizabeth, her kins-woman, who by God's favour is already six months pregnant with John the Baptist.

> "Elizabeth said: 'Of all women you are the most blessed, and blessed is the fruit of your womb. Why should I be honoured with a visit from the mother of my Lord? Look, the moment your greeting reached my ears, the child in my womb leapt for joy. Yes, blessed is she who believed that the promise made her by the Lord would be fulfilled.'"

Luke 2: 42-45

Are you hastening toward your heavenly home?

3. The Birth of Jesus

Our Blessed Lord, identifying with the poorest and humblest of his people, is born in a stable, while the angels announce to simple shepherds that man and God are reconciled.

> "The Word became flesh, he lived among us, and we saw his glory, the glory that he has from the Father as only Son of the Father, full of grace and truth."
>
> *John 1: 14*

4. The Presentation

In fulfilment of the law, Mary brings her first-born son to the Temple to acknowledge him as a gift from God. There, Simeon, inspired by the Holy Spirit, recognises him as the Light of the World.

> "My eyes have seen the salvation which you have made ready in the sight of the nations; a light of revelation for the gentiles, and glory for your people Israel."
>
> *Luke 2: 30-32*

It is high time for us to arise from sleep.

5. The Finding in the Temple

By the age of twelve, Jesus understands that doing the work of the Father is always going to be more important than any other duty. The gifts of reverence, and understanding of scripture show how much the Holy Spirit rested on him.

"Why were you looking for me? Did you not
know that I must be in my Father's house?'
But they did not understand what he meant."

Luke 2: 49-50

If you hear his voice today, do not harden your hearts.

THE FIVE SORROWFUL MYSTERIES

1. The Agony in the Garden

Our Lord, oppressed by sorrow, betrayed by one of his chosen companions, waiting to be arrested and led to death, turns to heartfelt prayer, and accepts whatever is the Father's will.

> "'Father,' he said, 'if you are willing, take this cup away from me. Nevertheless let your will be done, not mine.' In his anguish he prayed even more earnestly, and his sweat fell to the ground like great drops of blood."

Luke 22: 42, 44

2. The Scourging at the Pillar

Bound and helpless, though innocent, Jesus endures pain and humiliation, so that ever afterwards he can be a High Priest who has compassion with our darkest moments.

> "After having Jesus scourged, Pilate handed him over to be crucified."

Matthew 27: 26

Come and listen to me, my sons; I will teach you the fear of the Lord.

3. The Crowning with Thorns

Intending only mockery, Pilate's soldiers produce one of the finest symbols of our faith - a Saviour King, crowned with sorrow for our sins.

> "And they stripped him and put a scarlet cloak round him, and having twisted some thorns into a crown they put this on his head and placed a reed in his right hand. To make fun of him they knelt to him saying, 'Hail, king of the Jews!'"
>
> *Matthew 27: 28-29*

4. Jesus Carries his Cross

Jesus, the Paschal victim, bears the wood of the sacrifice like a priest. On the way he meets many people who, one way or another, find a way to share his suffering.

> "If anyone wants to be a follower of mine, let him renounce himself and take up his cross every day and follow me."
>
> *Luke 9: 23*

Is there anyone here who yearns for life and desires to see good days?

5. *The Crucifixion*

Jesus, the Sinless One, takes on himself the punishment for sin so that we might be forgiven. The Immortal One wrestles with Death so that we may have the fullness of Life.

> "Jesus gave a loud cry and breathed his last. And the veil of the Sanctuary was torn in two from top to bottom. The centurion, who was standing in front of him, had seen how he had died, and he said, 'In truth, this man was a Son of God.'"

Mark 15: 37-39

Keep your tongue free from all deceit.

THE FIVE GLORIOUS MYSTERIES

1. The Resurrection

By rising from the dead, Jesus shows himself to be truly the Holy One of God, and reveals to us that human nature is destined for life eternal with him, the first fruits of all those who have died.

> "'Why look among the dead for someone who is alive? He is not here; he has risen. Remember what he told you when he was still in Galilee - that the Son of man was destined to be handed over into the power of sinful men and be crucified, and rise again on the third day.'"

Luke 24: 5-7

2. The Ascension

When he ascends to heaven, Jesus finally enters into the glory of the victorious, risen Lord, and where he goes, the Church will follow, since the Church is his body, and he is its Head.

Turn away from evil and do good.

"May he enlighten the eyes of your mind so that you can see what hope his call holds for you, how rich is the glory of the heritage he offers among his holy people, and how extraordinarily great is the power that he has exercised for us believers; this accords with the strength of his power at work in Christ, the power which he exercised in raising him from the dead and enthroning him at his right hand, in heaven."

Ephesians 1: 18-21

3. The Descent of the Holy Spirit at Pentecost

When the Holy Spirit comes down on the disciples it transforms them, turning them into courageous witnesses to the resurrection. The Church still teaches and acts with the power of the Spirit, given to every member through faith and the sacraments of baptism and confirmation.

"They were all filled with the Holy Spirit and began to speak different languages as the Spirit gave them power to express themselves."

Acts 2: 4

Let peace be your quest and aim.

4. The Glorious Assumption of Our Lady

At the point of death, Mary is taken up, body and soul, into heaven to share her Son's glory, and as a Mother, to intercede for the human race.

> "Now I am going to tell you a mystery: we are not all going to fall asleep, but we are all going to be changed, instantly in the twinkling of an eye... this perishable nature of ours must put on imperishability, this mortal nature must put on immortality."

1 Corinthians 15: 51

5. The Coronation of Our Lady as Queen of Heaven

Closest to Christ in charity, faith and obedience, Mary, the humble daughter of Zion, is raised to the highest dignity in the Kingdom, and becomes the most glorious member of the communion of saints. As Queen of Heaven she continually praises God and prays for us sinners that, redeemed and sanctified, we may rejoice with her.

> "Now a great sign appeared in heaven: a woman, robed with the sun, standing on the moon, and on her head a crown of twelve stars."

Revelation 12: 1

Even before you ask me, I will say to you: Here I am.

PRAYERS TO OUR LADY

The Memorare

Remember, O most loving Virgin Mary, that it is a thing unheard of, that anyone ever had recourse to your protection, implored your help, or sought your intercession, and was left forsaken. Filled therefore with confidence in your goodness I fly to you, O Mother, Virgin of virgins. To you I come, before you I stand, a sorrowful sinner. Despise not my poor words, O Mother of the Word of God, but graciously hear and grant my prayer.

The Angelus

The angel of the Lord declared to Mary;
And she conceived of the Holy Spirit.
    Hail Mary, …
Behold the handmaid of the Lord;
Be it done to me according to your word.
    Hail Mary, …
And the Word was made flesh;
And dwelt among us.
    Hail Mary, …
Pray for us, O holy Mother of God;
That we may be made worthy of the promises of Christ.

Not to us, Lord, not to us give the glory, but to your name alone.

Let us pray: Pour forth, we beseech you, O Lord, your grace into our hearts that we, to whom the incarnation of Christ your Son, was made known by the message of an angel may be brought by his passion and cross to the glory of his resurrection, through the same Christ our Lord. Amen.

The Church's oldest Prayer to Our Lady

O Mother of God
we take refuge
in your loving care.
Let not our plea to you pass unheeded
in the trials that beset us,
but deliver us from danger,
for you alone
are truly pure,
you alone
are truly blessed.

(Translation of the Greek from which the prayer Sub tuum praesidium is derived)

Do you not know that the patience of God is leading you to repent?

The Magnificat

Magnificat anima mea Dominum;
Et exultavit spiritus meus in Deo salutari meo.
Quia respexit humilitatem ancillæ suæ;
ecce enim ex hoc beatam me dicent
omnes generationes.
Quia fecit mihi magna, qui potens est;
et sanctum nomen eius.
Et misericordia eius a progenie in progenies
timentibus eum.
Fecit potentiam in brachio suo;
dispersit superbos mente cordis sui.
Deposuit potentes de sede, et exaltavit humiles.
Esurientes implevit bonis;
et divites dimisit inanes.
Suscepit Israel puerum suum,
recordatus misericordiæ suæ.
Sicut locutus est ad patres nostros,
Abraham et semini eius in sæcula.

I do not wish the death of the sinner, but that he turn back to me and live.

The Magnificat

My soul glorifies the Lord;
my spirit rejoices in God, my Saviour.
He looks on his servant in her nothingness;
henceforth all ages will call me blessed.
The Almighty works marvels for me.
Holy his name!
His mercy is from age to age,
on those who fear him.
He puts forth his arm in strength
and scatters the proud-hearted.
He casts the mighty from their thrones
and raises the lowly.
He fills the starving with good things,
sends the rich away empty.
He protects Israel his servant,
remembering his mercy,
the mercy promised to our fathers,
to Abraham and his sons for ever.

*You have received the spirit of adoption of sons by which we
exclaim, Abba, father.*

MARIAN ANTIPHONS

Alma Redemptoris Mater

Alma Redemptoris Mater, quae pervia coeli
Porta manes, et stella maris, succurre cadenti
Surgere qui curat populo; tu quae genuisti,
Natura mirante, tuum sanctum Genitorem,
Virgo prius ac posterius, Gabrielis ab ore
Sumens illud Ave, peccatorum miserere.

Ave Regina Caelorum

Ave Regina coelorum,
Ave Domina Angelorum;
Salve radix, salve porta,
Ex qua mundo lux est orta;
Gaude, Virgo gloriosa,
Super omnes speciosa;
Vale O valde decora,
Et pro nobis Christum exora.

Regina Caeli Laetare

Regina coeli, laetare, alleluia,
Quia quem meruisti portare, alleluia,
Resurrexit, sicut dixit, alleluia,
Ora pro nobis Deum, alleluia.

---

*Seek first the kingdom of God and his justice, and all these
things will be given you as well.*

Alma Redemptoris Mater

Mother of Christ, hear your people's cry.
Star of the sea and portal of the sky.
Sinking we strive and call to you for aid,
Mother of him who you from nothing made.
Oh by that joy which Gabriel brought to you,
you virgin first and last
let us your mercy see.

Ave Regina Caelorum

Hail O Queen of heav'n enthroned,
Hail by angels Mistress owned,
Root of Jesse, Gate of morn,
whence the world's true Light was born.
Glorious Virgin joy to thee,
loveliest whom in heav'n they see,
fairest thou where all are fair
plead with Christ our sins to spare.

Regina Caeli Laetare

O Queen of heaven rejoice; Alleluia.
For he whom thou didst merit to bear; Alleluia.
Has risen as he said; Alleluia.
Pray for us to God; Alleluia.

Those who fear him lack nothing.

Salve Regina

Salve, Regina, Mater misericordiae;
vita, dulcedo et spes nostra, salve.
Ad te clamamus exsules filii Hevae.
Ad te suspiramus gementes et flentes
in hac lacrimarum valle. Eia ergo,
advocata nostra, illos tuos misericordes
oculos ad nos converte. Et Jesum,
benedictum fructum ventris tui,
nobis post hoc exsilium ostende.
O clemens, o pia, o dulcis Virgo Maria.

Renounce yourself in order to follow Christ.

Salve Regina

Hail, holy Queen, Mother of Mercy,
hail our life our sweetness and our hope;
to thee do we cry, poor banished children of Eve;
to thee do we send up our sighs,
mourning and weeping in this vale of tears.
Turn then, most gracious advocate,
thine eyes of mercy towards us;
and after this our exile show unto us
the blessed fruit of thy womb, Jesus.
O clement, O loving, O sweet Virgin Mary.

Do not repay one bad turn with another.

PRAYERS FOR THE SICK

God our Father,
your Son accepted our sufferings
to teach us the virtue of patience in human illness.
Hear the prayers we offer for our sick brother/sister.
May all who suffer pain, illness, or disease
realize that they have been chosen to be saints
and know that they are joined to Christ in his
suffering for the salvation of the world.
We ask this through Christ our Lord. Amen.

Father in heaven, grant N comfort in his/her suffering.
Give him/her courage, when afraid,
Give him/her patience, when afflicted,
Give him/her hope, when dejected,
And when alone assure him/her of
the prayerful support of your holy people.
We ask this through Christ Our Lord.

Prayer for a sick child

God of love,
ever caring, ever strong,
stand by us in our time of need.
Watch over your child N. who is sick,
look after him/her in every danger,
and grant him/her your healing and peace.
We ask this in the name of Jesus the Lord.

---

*The eye has not seen, nor the ear heard what God has
prepared for those who love him.*

COMMENDATION
OF THE DYING

One or more of the following short texts may be recited with the dying person. If necessary, they may be softly repeated two or three times.

Who can separate us from the love of Christ?

Romans 8: 35

Whether we live or die, we are the Lord's.

Romans 14: 8

Though I walk in the shadow of death,
I will fear no evil,
for you are with me.

Psalm 22: 4

Into your hands, O Lord, I commend my spirit.
Lord Jesus receive my soul
Jesus. Jesus, Jesus.

Jesus, Mary and Joseph, I give you my heart and my soul.
Jesus, Mary and Joseph, assist me in my last agony.
Jesus, Mary and Joseph, may I breathe forth my soul in peace with you.

Narrow is the road that leads to life.

155

Litany of the Saints

When the condition of the dying person calls for the use of brief forms of prayer, those who are present are encouraged to pray the Litany of the Saints - or at least some of its invocations. (See page 163)

Reading   *John 14: 1-6, 23, 27*

Jesus says:
"Do not let your hearts be troubled.
Trust in God still, and trust in me.
There are many rooms in my Father's house;
if there were not, I should have told you.
I am going now to prepare a place for you,
and after I have gone and prepared you a place,
I shall return to take you with me;
so that where I am
you may be too."

Prayer of Commendation

When the moment of death seems near, the following prayer should be recited:

Go forth, O Christian soul, out of this world, in the name of God the Father almighty, who created you; in the name of Jesus Christ, the Son of the living God, who suffered for you; in the name of the Holy Spirit, who was given to you; in the name of the holy and glorious Mary, Virgin Mother of God; in the name of

---

In a flood of words you will not avoid sin.

156

blessed Joseph; in the name of the angels, archangels, thrones and dominations; in the name of the patriarchs and prophets, of the holy apostles and evangelists, of the holy martyrs, confessors, monks and hermits, of the holy virgins, and of all the saints of God; may peace be yours this day, and may your home be in heaven. Through the same Christ our Lord. Amen.

I commend you, my dear brother/sister,
to almighty God,
and entrust you to your Creator.
May you return to him
who formed you from the dust of the earth.
May holy Mary, the angels, and all the saints
come to meet you as you go forth from this life.
May Christ who was crucified for you
bring you freedom and peace.
May Christ who died for you
admit you into his garden of paradise.
May Christ, the true Shepherd,
acknowledge you as one of his flock.
May he forgive all your sins,
and set you among those he has chosen.
May you see your Redeemer face to face,
and enjoy the vision of God for ever. Amen.
The Hail Holy Queen (see page 153) may be recited at this point.

The tongue holds the key to life and death.

Prayer after Death

Saints of God, come to his/her aid!
Come to meet him/her, angels of the Lord!
Receive his/her soul and present him/her to God the
Most High.
May Christ, who called you, take you to himself;
may angels lead you to Abraham's side.
Lord, grant him/her eternal rest,
and may your light shine upon him/her for ever.

Psalm 129 (see page 75) is then recited.

Prayer for the family and friends

God of mercy,
into your hands we commend our brother/sister.
We are confident that
with all who have died in Christ
he/she will be raised to life on the last day
and live with Christ for ever.
Lord, hear our prayer:
welcome our brother/sister to paradise
and help us to comfort each other
with the assurances of faith
until we all meet in Christ
to be with you and with our brother/sister for ever.
We ask this through Christ our Lord. Amen.

God searches hearts and minds.

PRAYERS FOR THE DEAD

Let us pray.
Loving and merciful God,
we entrust our brother/sister to your mercy.
You loved him/her greatly in this life;
now that he/she is freed from all its cares,
give him/her happiness and peace for ever.
The old order has passed away;
welcome him/her now into paradise
where there will be no more sorrow,
no more weeping or pain,
but only peace and joy
with Jesus, your Son,
and the Holy Spirit
for ever and ever.
Amen.

Reading
John 14: 1-6,23,27.

Jesus says:
"Do not let your hearts be troubled.
Trust in God still, and trust in me.
There are many rooms in my Father's house;
if there were not, I should have told you.

---

*There are ways which men call right that in the end plunge
into the depths of hell.*

I am going now to prepare a place for you,
and after I have gone and prepared you a place,
I shall return to take you with me;
so that where I am you may be too.
You know the way to the place where I am going."
Thomas said, "Lord, we do not know where you are
going, so how can we know the way?" Jesus said:
"I am the Way, the Truth and the Life.
No one can come to the Father except through me.
If anyone loves me he will keep my word,
and my Father will love him,
and we shall come to him
and make our home with him.
Peace I bequeath to you,
my own peace I give you,
a peace the world cannot give, this is my gift to you.
Do not let your hearts be troubled or afraid."

Litany

Saints of God, come to his/her aid!
Come to meet him/her, angels of the Lord!

Holy Mary, Mother of God	pray for him/her
Saint Joseph	pray for him/her
Saint Peter and Paul	pray for him/her

Anyone who perseveres to the end will be saved.

The following prayer is added:

God of mercy,
hear our prayers and be merciful
to your son/daughter N., whom you have called from
this life.
Welcome him/her into the company of your saints,
in the kingdom of light and peace.
We ask this through Christ our Lord.
Amen.

Let us pray for the coming of the kingdom as Jesus
taught us:

> Our Father ...

> Hail Mary ...

> Glory be to the Father ...

Prayer of Commendation

Lord Jesus, our Redeemer,
you willingly gave yourself up to death
so that all people might be saved
and pass from death into a new life.
Listen to our prayers,
look with love on your people
who mourn and pray for their brother/sister N.

Eternal rest grant unto him/her, O Lord
and let perpetual light fall upon him/her.
May he/she rest in peace. Amen.

Be brave of heart and rely on the Lord.

Anima Christi
(See page 92)

We seem to give them back to you O God who gave them to us. Yet as you did not lose them in giving, so do we not lose them by their return. Not as the world gives, do you give, O Lover of souls. What you give you do not take away, for what is yours is ours also if we are yours. And life is eternal and love immortal, and death is only an horizon, and an horizon is nothing save the limit of our sight. Lift us up, strong Son of god, that we may see further; cleanse our eyes that we may see more clearly; draw us closer to yourself that we may know ourselves to be nearer to our loved ones who are with you. And while you prepare a place for us, prepare us also for that happy place, that where you are we may also be for evermore.

Make known your way to the Lord and hope in him.

Litany of the Saints

Lord have mercy.
Christ have mercy.
Lord have mercy.

Holy Mary, Mother of God   pray for us.
Saint Michael
Holy angels of God
Saint John the Baptist
Saint Joseph
Saint Peter and Saint Paul
Saint Andrew
Saint John
Saint Mary Magdalene
Saint Stephen
Saint Ignatius
Saint Laurence
Saint John Fisher and Saint Thomas More
Saint Perpetua and Saint Felicity
Saint Agnes
Saint Gregory
Saint Ambrose
Saint Augustine
Saint Athanasius
Saint Anthony
Saint Pachomius
Saint Basil
Saint Martin

---

*O God, come to my assistance. O Lord, make haste
to help me.*

LITANIES

Our Holy Father Saint Benedict
Saint Scholastica
Saint Maurus and Saint Placid
Saint Columba
Saint Augustine of Canterbury
Saint Aidan
Saint Cuthbert
Saint Benet Biscop
Saint Bede
Saint Bernard
Saint Aelred
Saint Francis and Saint Dominic
Saint Ignatius of Loyola
Saint Francis Xavier
Saint Alban Roe
Saint Vincent de Paul
Saint John Bosco
Saint John Vianney
Saint Gertrude
Saint Catherine
Saint Teresa of Avila
Saint Therese of Lisieux
All holy men and women
Lord be merciful   Lord save your people
From all evil
From every sin
From everlasting death

He who serves well secures a good standing for himself.

LITANIES

By your coming as man
By your death and rising to new life
By your gift of the Holy Spirit
Be merciful to us sinners   Lord hear our prayer
Guide and protect your holy Church
Keep the Pope and all the clergy in faithful service
to your Church
Bring all peoples together in trust and peace
Strengthen us in your service
Jesus, Son of the living God
Christ hear us
Christ hear us.

Everyone has his own gift from God.

LITANIES

Litany of the Blessed Virgin

Kyrie eleison.
Christe eleison.
Kyrie eleison.
Christe audi nos.
Christe exaudi nos.
Pater de cælis Deus, miserere nobis.
Fili Redemptor mundi Deus, miserere nobis.
Spiritus Sancte Deus, miserere nobis.
Sancta Trinitas, unus Deus, miserere nobis.
Sancta Maria, ora pro nobis.
Sancta Dei genitrix,
Sancta Virgo virginum,
Mater Christi,
Mater Ecclesiae,
Mater divinæ gratiæ,
Mater purissima,
Mater castissima,
Mater inviolata,
Mater intermerata,
Mater amabilis,
Mater admirabilis,
Mater boni consilii,
Mater Creatoris,
Mater Salvatoris,
Virgo prudentissima,
Virgo veneranda,
Virgo prædicanda,
Virgo potens,
Virgo clemens,

Litany of the Blessed Virgin

Lord, have mercy on us.
Christ have mercy on us.
Lord, have mercy on us.
Christ, hear us.
Christ, graciously hear us.
God the Father, of heaven, have mercy on us.
God the Son, Redeemer of the world, have mercy on us.
God the Holy Ghost, have mercy on us.
Holy Trinity, one God, have mercy on us.
Holy Mary, pray for us.
Holy Mother of God,
Holy Virgin of virgins,
Mother of Christ,
Mother of the Church,
Mother of divine grace,
Mother most pure,
Mother most chaste,
Mother inviolate,
Mother undefiled,
Mother most loving,
Mother most admirable,
Mother of good counsel,
Mother of our Creator,
Mother of our Saviour,
Virgin most prudent,
Virgin most venerable,
Virgin most renowned,
Virgin most powerful,
Virgin most merciful,

LITANIES

Virgo fidelis,
Speculum justitiæ,
Sedes sapientiæ,
Causa nostræ lætitiæ,
Vas spirituale,
Vas honorabile,
Vas insigne devotionis,
Rosa mystica,
Turris Davidica,
Turris eburnea,
Domus aurea,
Fœderis arca,
Janua cæli,
Stella matutina,
Salus infirmorum,
Refugium peccatorum,
Consolatrix afflictorum,
Auxilium Christianorum,
Regina angelorum,
Regina patriarcharum,
Regina prophetarum,
Regina apostolorum,
Regina martyrum,
Regina confessorum,
Regina virginum,
Regina sanctorum omnium,
Regina sine labe originali concepta,
Regina in cælum assumpta,
Regina sacratissimi rosarii,
Regina pacis, ora pro nobis.

Virgin most faithful,
Mirror of justice,
Seat of wisdom,
Cause of our joy,
Spiritual vessel,
Vessel of honour,
Singular vessel of devotion,
Mystical rose,
Tower of David,
Tower of ivory,
House of gold,
Ark of the covenant,
Gate of heaven,
Morning star,
Health of the weak,
Refuge of sinners,
Comforter of the afflicted,
Help of Christians,
Queen of angels,
Queen of patriarchs,
Queen of prophets,
Queen of apostles,
Queen of martyrs,
Queen of confessors,
Queen of virgins,
Queen of all saints,
Queen conceived without original sin,
Queen assumed into heaven,
Queen of the most holy rosary,
Queen of of peace, pray for us.

LITANIES

Agnus Dei, qui tollis peccata mundi,
    parce nobis, Domine.
Agnus Dei, qui tollis peccata mundi,
    exaudi nos, Domine.
Agnus Dei, qui tollis peccata mundi,
    miserere nobis.

V. Ora pro nobis, sancta Dei Genitrix,
R. Ut digni efficiamur promissionibus Christi.

Oremus:

Concede nos famulos tuos, quæsumus Domine Deus,
perpetua mentis et corporis sanitate gaudere;
et gloriosa beatæ Mariæ semper Virginis intercessione
a præsenti liberari tristitia et æterna perfrui lætitia.
Per Christum Dominum nostrum. Amen.

LITANIES

Lamb of God, who takest away the sins of the world,
spare us, O Lord.
Lamb of God, who takest away the sins of the world,
graciously hear us, O Lord.
Lamb of God, who takest away the sins of the world,
have mercy on us.

V. Pray for us, O holy Mother of God.
R. That we may be made worthy of the promises of
Christ.

Let us pray:

Grant, O Lord God, we beseech you, that we your
servants may enjoy constant health of body and mind,
and by the glorious intercession of blessed Mary ever
Virgin may be delivered from present sadness and
come to those joys that are eternal.
Through Christ our Lord. Amen.

Veni Creator Spiritus

Veni, Creator Spiritus,
Mentes tuorum visita;
Imple superna gratia
Quæ tu creasti pectora.

Qui Paraclitus diceris,
Donum Dei altissimi,
Fons vivus, ignis, caritas
Et spiritalis unctio.

Tu septiformis munere,
Dextræ Dei tu digitus,
Tu rite promissum Patris
Sermone ditans guttura.

Accende lumen sensibus,
Infunde amorem cordibus,
Infirma nostri corporis
Virtute firmans perpeti.

Hostem repellas longius
Pacemque dones protinus;
Ductore sic te prævio
Vitemus omne noxium.

Per te sciamus da Patrem
Noscamus atque Filium;
te utriusque Spiritum
Credamus omni tempore.

Gloria Patri Domino
Natoque qui a mortuis
Surrexit ac Paraclito
In sæculorum sæcula.

Veni Creator Spiritus

Come, creator Spirit,
visit the souls of your people;
fill with the grace of heaven
the hearts that you have made.

You who are called friend to us,
gift of the most high God,
the spring of life, of fire, of love,
the anointing of the soul.

Sevenfold the gifts you touch us with,
finger of God's right hand,
you are the Father's promise kept,
blessing our tongues in prayer.

Kindle your light for our senses,
pour love into our hearts,
make strong our bodies' weakness
with your unfailing strength.

Drive Satan far away from us
and give us lasting peace;
so that, with you our lord and guide,
no harm may come to us.

Through you may we know God our Father
and learn to know his Son;
and you, the Spirit of them both,
may we believe always.

Glory be given to God the Father,
to God the Son who rose
from death, and to you, Holy Spirit, now
and for all time to come.

Veni Sancte Spiritus

Veni, Sancte Spiritus,
Et emitte cælitus
Lucis tuæ radium.

Veni pater pauperum,
Veni dator munerum,
Veni lumen cordium.

Consolator optime,
Dulcis hospes animæ,
Dulce refrigerium.

In labore requies,
In æstu temperies,
In fletu solatium.

O lux beatissima,
Reple cordis intima
Tuorum fidelium.

Sine tuo numine
Nihil est in homine,
Nihil est innoxium.

Lava quod est sordidum,
Riga quod est aridum,
Sana quod est saucium,

Flecte quod est rigidum,
Fove quod est frigidum,
Rege quod est devium.

Veni Sancte Spiritus

Come, Holy Spirit,
and send from heaven
the ray of your light.

Come, father of the poor;
come, giver of gifts;
come, light of hearts.

Best consoler,
sweet guest of the soul,
sweet refreshment,

In hard work rest,
in the heat coolness,
in grief consolation,

O most blessed light,
fill the inmost hearts
of your faithful people.

Without your power
nothing is (good) in man,
nothing is innocent.

Wash what is fouled,
water what is dry,
heal what is wounded;

Bend what is stiff,
warm what is cold,
straighten what is crooked.

Da tuis fidelibus
In te confidentibus
Sacrum septenarium;

Da virtutis meritum,
Da salutis exitum,
Da perenne gaudium.

Te Deum Laudamus

Te Deum laudamus; te Dominum confitemur.
Te æternum Patrem omnis terra veneratur.
Tibi omnes angeli, tibi cæli et universæ potestates,
Tibi Cherubim et Seraphim
incessabili voce proclamant:
Sanctus, Sanctus, Sanctus, Dominus Deus sabaoth;
Pleni sunt cæli et terra majestatis gloriæ tuæ.
Te gloriosus apostolorum chorus,
Te prophetarum laudabilis numerus,
Te martyrum candidatus laudat exercitus.
Te per orbem terrarum sancta confitetur Ecclesia
Patrem immensæ majestatis,
Venerandum tuum verum et unicum Filium,
Sanctum quoque Paraclitum Spiritum.
Tu rex gloriæ, Christe:
Tu Patris sempiternus es Filius.

Give to your faithful people
whose trust is in you
your seven holy things.

Give the reward of goodness,
give salvation as our end
give everlasting joy.

Te Deum Laudamus

We praise you, O God; we acclaim you as the Lord.
Everlasting Father,
all the world bows down before you.
All the angels sing your praise,
the hosts of heaven and all the angel powers,
all the cherubim and seraphim call out to you
in unending song:
Holy, Holy, Holy, is the Lord God of angel hosts!
The heavens and the earth are filled
with your majesty and glory.
The glorious band of apostles,
the noble company of prophets, the white-robed army
who shed their blood for Christ,
all sing your praises.
And to the ends of the earth
your holy Church proclaims her faith in you.
Father, whose majesty is boundless,
your true and only Son, who is to be adored,
the Holy Spirit sent to be our advocate.
You, O Christ, are the King of glory,
Son of the eternal Father.

Tu ad liberandum suscepturus hominem,
non horruisti Virginis uterum.
Tu devicto mortis aculeo
aperuisti credentibus regna cælorum.
Tu ad dexteram Dei sedes, in gloria Patris.
Judex crederis esse venturus.
Te ergo quæsumus, tuis famulis subveni,
quos pretioso Sanguine redemisti.
Aeterna fac cum sanctis tuis in gloria numerari.
Salvum fac populum tuum, Domine,
et benedic hæreditati tuæ.
Et rege eos et extolle illos usque in æternum.
Per singulos dies benedicimus te,
Et laudamus nomen tuum in sæculum
et in sæculum sæculi.
Dignare, Domine, die isto sine peccato nos custodire.
Miserere nostri, Domine, miserere nostri.
Fiat misericordia tua, Domine, super nos,
quemadmodum speravimus in te.
In te, Domine, speravi; non confundar in æternum.

When you took our nature to save mankind
you did not shrink from birth in the Virgin's womb.
You overcame the power of death
opening the Father's kingdom
to all who believe in you.
Enthroned at God's right hand
in the glory of the Father,
you will come in judgment
according to your promise.
You redeemed your people by your precious blood.
Come, we implore you, to our aid.
Grant us with the saints a place in glory everlasting.
Lord, save your people and bless your inheritance.
Rule them and uphold them for ever and ever.
Day by day we praise you;
we acclaim you now and to all eternity.
In your goodness, Lord, keep us free from sin.
Have mercy on us, Lord, have mercy.
May your mercy always be with us, Lord,
for we have hoped in you.
In you, Lord, we put our trust:
we shall not be put to shame.

The Benedictus may be said at the end of each day's Morning Prayers

Benedictus

Benedictus Dominus Deus Israel;
quia visitavit, et fecit redemptionem plebis suae.
Et erexit cornu salutis nobis in domo David pueri sui.
Sicut locutus est per os sanctorum,
qui a saeculo sunt, prophetarum ejus.
Salutem ex inimicis nostris;
et de manu omnium, qui oderunt nos.
Ad faciendam misericordiam cum patribus nostris;
et memorari testamenti sui sancti.
Jusjurandum, quod juravit ad Abraham patrem
nostrum, daturum se nobis.
Ut sine timore, de manu inimicorum nostrorum
liberati, serviamus illi.
In sanctitate et justitia coram ipso,
omnibus diebus nostris.
Et tu puer, propheta Altissimmi vocaberis;
praeibis enim ante faciem Domini parare vias ejus;
Ad dandam scientiam salutis plebi ejus,
in remissionem peccatorum eorum;
Per viscera misericordiae Dei nostri,
in quibus visitavit nos Oriens ex alto;
Illuminare his, qui in tenebris
et in umbra mortis sedent;
ad dirigendos pedes nostros in viam pacis.

Benedictus

Blessed be the Lord, the God of Israel;
he has come to his people and set them free.
He has raised up for us a mighty saviour,
born of the house of his servant David.

Through his holy prophets he promised of old
that he would save us from our enemies,
from the hands of all who hate us.
He promised to show mercy to our fathers
and to remember his holy covenant.

This was the oath he swore to our father Abraham:
to set us free from the hand of our enemies,
free to worship him without fear,
holy and righteous in his sight all the days of our life.

You, my child, shall be called
the prophet of the Most High
for you will go before the Lord to prepare his way,
to give his people knowledge of salvation
by forgiving them their sins.

In the tender compassion of our God
the dawn from on high shall break upon us,
to shine on those who dwell in darkness
and the shadow of death,
and to guide our feet on the road of peace.

Ad S. Benedictum

Terras per omnes qui venerabilis
Gaudes paterno nomine, te patrem
    Dixere, qui nostras in oras
        Signa tulere fidemque Christi.

Te laeta quondam turba fidelium
Nostris in arvis templa per omnia
    Te ture multo, te colebat
        Vocibus adsiduis patronum.

Crebris et arae lampadibus nitent
Dum fana notam rite sonant precem
    'Tu sisque felix sopitesque
        Sancte tuam Benedicte gentem'.

Stat prisca nostris pectoribus fides;
Te sempiternis laudibus inclitum
    Nos efferemus, te perenni
        Carmine concelebrent nepotes.

---

*Receive me, Lord, as you have promised, and I shall live; do
not disappoint me in my hope.*

Hymn to Saint Benedict

Our blessed father, Benedict,
Sure guide in dark and troubled days,
Has shown his countless children here
The paths of peace, the Lord's own ways.

He dwelt in heaven while on earth,
True man of God and man of prayer;
For him, the love of Christ was all
And God was present everywhere.

21st March
He died among his many sons
While lifting up his hands to pray;
In glory clothed, he lives again
Whose monks rejoice in him today.

11th July
He left all things that bind the heart,
In poverty to find release;
Unmoved among the things that change,
He sought and found a lasting peace.

Now Benedict, with all his sons
Around him, like a crown of gold,
Gives praise to you blest Trinity,
In splendid light and time untold.

---

*Never do to another what you would not want done to
yourself.*

INDEX OF PRAYERS

INDEX OF PRAYERS

INDEX OF PRAYERS

INDEX OF PRAYERS

INDEX OF PRAYERS

INDEX OF PSALMS